THE VIGILANT CITIZEN

The Vigilant Citizen

Everyday Policing and Insecurity in Miami

Thijs Jeursen

NEW YORK UNIVERSITY PRESS
New York

NEW YORK UNIVERSITY PRESS
New York
www.nyupress.org

© 2023 by New York University
All rights reserved

Library of Congress Cataloging-in-Publication Data
Names: Jeursen, Thijs Jonathan, author.
Title: The vigilant citizen : everyday policing and insecurity in Miami / Thijs Jeursen.
Description: New York : New York University Press, [2022] |
Includes bibliographical references and index.
Identifiers: LCCN 2022014013 | ISBN 9781479816538 (hardback ; alk. paper) |
ISBN 9781479816545 (paperback ; alk. paper) | ISBN 9781479816552 (ebook) |
ISBN 9781479816569 (ebook other)
Subjects: LCSH: Police—Florida—Miami. | Police-community relations—Florida—Miami. | Miami (Fla.)—Race relations. | Miami (Fla.)—Social conditions.
Classification: LCC HV8148.M43 J48 2022 | DDC 363.2/309759381—dc23/eng/20220610
LC record available at https://lccn.loc.gov/2022014013

New York University Press books are printed on acid-free paper, and their binding materials are chosen for strength and durability. We strive to use environmentally responsible suppliers and materials to the greatest extent possible in publishing our books.

Manufactured in the United States of America

10 9 8 7 6 5 4 3 2 1

Also available as an ebook

CONTENTS

List of Figures — vii

Introduction: At the End of the Day Everybody Goes Home — 1

1. Places and Partnerships of Policing — 33

2. Do the Right Thing — 63

3. Guns for the Good Guys — 95

4. Looking through the Law — 121

Conclusion: American Values? — 145

Acknowledgments — 157

Notes — 161

Bibliography — 163

Index — 171

About the Author — 179

LIST OF FIGURES

Figure I.1. The Miami Beach police station on Washington Avenue, March 2015.   1

Figure I.2. The names Demz, Reefa, Trayvon Martin, and M. Brown on a mural tombstone in Wynwood, April 2015.   9

Figure 1.1. "Hire Overtown, End Segregation," March 2015.   33

Figure 1.2. Map of Miami, including the locations of Wynwood, Overtown, and South Beach.   38

Figure 1.3. Memorial Day weekend 2015 traffic and security pattern, May 2015. Source: City of Miami Beach.   58

Figure 2.1. Miami Police Department police officers look for information after the murder of Marlon Eason in Overtown, March 2015.   63

Figure 2.2. A "ticket citation" from the Miami Police Department providing free pizza, August 2015.   74

Figure 2.3. Crime-watch meeting organized by Alejandra (not in picture), May 2015.   78

Figure 2.4. Document distributed after the murder of Marlon Eason, March 2015. Source: Miami Police Department.   82

Figure 2.5. Vigil after the murder of Marlon Eason, March 2015.   87

Figure 3.1. Street in the neighborhood where Olaf and I lived in 2015, February 2015. 94

Figure 3.2. Sign on the front door of a gun store in Wynwood, March 2015. 104

Figure 4.1. Mural in Wynwood, October 2016. 120

Figure c.1. "Trump does not represent American values," October 2016. 145

Introduction

At the End of the Day Everybody Goes Home

The first time I joined a Miami police officer for a ride-along, I opted for a patrol in Miami Beach on a Friday night. As the city is internationally known for its nightlife and entertainment, I figured that a weekend night between 10 p.m. and 8 a.m. in Miami Beach would give me an interesting and diverse experience of police work in the city. After signing multiple waivers and legal documents—basically declaring that the police department could not be held liable if I sustained any injury or died during the ride-along—I arrived at the police station an hour early, walked around outside for a bit, and took the photo shown in figure I.1.

I was eventually guided upstairs, where I was asked to sit at a desk in a cubicle and wait for the patrol officer to pick me up. Trying to follow

Figure I.1. The Miami Beach police station on Washington Avenue, March 2015.

the official dress code for "civilian observers," I wore formal business attire with slightly pointy-toed gray leather shoes. I could not see any officers present in the office, but I overheard them talking about my appearance. As a relatively tall man dressed in clothes I had brought from the Netherlands, I immediately stood out, and two officers joked that I had on "clown shoes." I was unsure whether I was supposed to hear this banter or not. They peeked around the cubicle and greeted me, interested to know who I was and why I wanted to accompany a patrol officer in Miami, so far away from home. My name, quite uncommon in the United States, was difficult for them to pronounce, but they could rhyme it: I was "Thijs-double-nice."[1]

"Europe, eh?" Officer Hernandez[2] summarized my response after I told him I lived in the Netherlands. "So, how do you protect yourself, when, you know, you're in danger?" I had no direct answer to his question and asked for a bit of context, to which he expressed his concerns about a growing Muslim population in Europe, a population that, according to him, posed a grave threat to national security and the safety of citizens. He also referred to terror incidents in major cities. Somewhat perplexed by the bluntness of his question, I mumbled something along the lines of "I just hope I won't be in the wrong place at the wrong time, that nobody targets me." Hernandez sniffed and gave me a tightlipped smile. I felt naive. "Boss," he addressed me, without any implied deference, "when I get in trouble, I have this." He began to unbutton his shirt, revealing a necklace with a leather case attached to it, decorated with a large Christian cross. It holstered a knife. "And these," he went on, removing another knife from a holster attached to his ankle, and yet a third from his belt. After returning the knives to their holsters and straightening his collar, he wished me a good evening and an eventful ride-along with the patrol officer.

It did indeed turn out to be quite an eventful ride-along, much like the many subsequent times I joined Miami police officers during patrol shifts. "Riding shotgun," or sitting alongside the driver (in Miami there is only one officer per police car), I was able to observe clearly how police officers do their work during patrol shifts. I was fortunate to become affiliated with two police departments in Miami with relative ease. One of my dissertation supervisors at the University of Amsterdam provided me with a contact at the Miami Beach Police Department (MBPD) through a friend of hers. And after I met various police officers at the Miami Police Department (MPD) during public meetings, these two departments accepted me as a researcher—though they often saw me as a student who had to write a paper for school, mostly because of how they understood my work (and, I'd like to think, because of my youthful appearance). In the end, I was able to join patrol officers at these departments during both day and night shifts for a total of one hundred hours.

These ride-alongs provided firsthand information on the relationships and interactions between police officers and residents, as well as between police officers themselves. I joined them as they chased cars with their sirens and flashing lights, arrested suspects, entered license plate numbers into the computer, broke up fistfights, searched for intruders, and responded to a diverse range of emergency calls, as well as when they talked to bouncers and security guards, and to residents in distress in various neighborhoods, while frequently checking license plates and criminal registrations. During quieter moments, I was also able to talk with them, and discuss hot-button issues such as police body cameras, police brutality, and their overall experiences of crime and safety in Miami.

Yet, to this day, I still find myself thinking about Officer Hernandez, who showed me his three knives before I had even set foot in a police car. This interaction, I came to realize, had much in common with many other discussions and encounters I had during my research on policing in Miami. This was an interaction not between primarily an officer and a visitor but one between citizens of different nations: an interaction in which one asked the other how he went about arranging his own protection, how he made use of the available rights and laws, and what responsibilities he felt in terms of his personal safety. As part of his police uniform, Officer Hernandez wore a fully equipped tactical belt, including firearm, Taser, two additional magazines, flashlight, and clip used to mount his smartphone. He also had a radio that enabled him to call his colleagues for backup. Yet he still felt the need or the desire to carry three additional knives for his personal safety. Why?

Drawn to global popular imaginaries of American crime, glamour, and inequality, I came to Miami to study the broader social and political concerns about police brutality and racial injustice that are part of the national conversation in the United States right now. Miami is a place where such inequalities have become particularly visible as well as contested. After my eleven months of fieldwork in the city, in which I drew on the stories and experiences of police officers, private security guards, neighborhood-watch groups, civil-society organizations, and a broad range of residents and activists, I concluded that ideas and feelings of insecurity and individual responsibility are pervasive throughout society. Rather than being exclusive to police officers, such sentiments, shared by diverse individuals and groups, relate to large-scale societal developments that can be understood in terms of citizenship. In truth, Officer Hernandez presented himself not so much as a police officer as a "vigilant citizen." The title of this book refers to an ideal type of citizen, one emblematic of "good citizenship." A vigilant citizen is someone who understands how to deal with insecurity, or who knows how and when they should defend themselves. Vigilant citizenship emphasizes that, as citizens, people themselves can and should deal with physical threats in everyday life. Such citizens take on this responsibility of self-defense and look to contribute to public safety, duties they often share with the police. As a security-specific iteration of neighboring concepts such as individualism and self-reliance, vigilant citizenship is about how policing goes beyond the police force and becomes a part of the way people understand their rights and roles as private citizens; it implies that citizens need to arrange for the security measures they deem necessary in a city characterized by high levels of crime and inequality. This book analyzes how vigilant citizenship is worked out and experienced in the everyday, where people strive to figure out how they can make use of weapons, technologies, and surveillance to feel and keep safe.

While I did not meet any other police officers who carried knives, it is easy to read Officer Hernandez's approach to protection as illustrative of the hyperviolent and racialized policing of cities across the United States. Much recent scholarship on urban security and policing has concentrated on police brutality, showing how in many contexts the police themselves are violent criminal actors who endanger rather than protect urban populations. Police brutality is generally understood as resulting from a racist and aggressive organizational culture within police forces. While scholarship on police brutality and institutionalized racism within police departments remains critical, it tends to overlook how a logic of individualized responsibility for security exacerbates and legitimizes existing inequalities. How, then, can we understand these inequalities associated with policing in ways that recognize but also go beyond police brutality?

In this book, I argue that precisely through its broader emphasis on individual rights and responsibilities, vigilant citizenship makes it harder for both policed citizens and policing actors to appreciate the systematic nature of racialized policing practices. As a central premise in everyday policing, vigilant citizenship frames racist and violent policing as matters of personal blame and individual guilt—as problems of citizens. This framing obscures the role of state institutions and market forces that have purposefully created and defended the structural conditions of inequality and white supremacy. Vigilant citizenship waters down the realities of how race operates in policing and US society more broadly.[3] It suggests that state-sanctioned violence and racialized policing are normative and legal questions of self-defense and personal protection, related to who "did the right thing" and who did not. Indeed, problems inherent to policing are still often believed to be solved with additional training programs and bureaucratic oversight, as well as the prosecution of individual officers. "Such individualist framings," as Jonathan Rosa and Vanessa Díaz also note, "suggest that racism is an exceptional, idiosyncratic phenomenon that can be eradicated through behavior-oriented interventions" (2019: 121).

Throughout this book, I use the lens of vigilant citizenship to analyze two aspects of policing. First, I explore the extent to which police officers and other policing actors themselves experience fear and react to insecurity in highly individualized ways. While police officers and security guards may use violence in their line of work, they also experience their working conditions as highly precarious and fraught with danger. For them, policing is about maintaining boundaries, about differentiating between good and bad guys, and between danger and safety—involving boundaries that are at the same time "unstable and full of contradictions."[4] Yet they do not necessarily expect their employers to protect them; they feel responsible for identifying and addressing these insecurities as individuals, and they align themselves with citizens and collectives who feel and act the same. Second, these individualized experiences and practices of policing extend beyond immediate encounters with policing professionals. Ideals of self-protection and of being vigilant, and thus of not necessarily being reliant on the police, can be associated with violent forms of legal and extralegal self-defense. Despite police officers' untouchability and their weapons, Officer Hernandez's approach to personal protection illustrates how police officers in general see themselves as at risk, too, like citizens. Unwittingly, he mobilized his racialized perception of Muslims and terrorist incidents to suggest that threats are all around us, justifying his own willingness to use violence in response. In his view, every citizen should do the same—whether you are a patrol officer in Miami or a university student in the Netherlands. Through the lens of vigilant citizenship, I seek to extend analyses of policing in and beyond police encounters, focusing on the oft-blurred boundaries between police officers and citizens in policing. These violent policing acts have proved to be racially inequitable in ways that parallel police brutality in the sense that they, too, disproportionally affect the lives of Black and nonwhite citizens whereas perpetrators still enjoy widespread support and are often found not guilty.

In the contexts of ubiquitous firearms and heated public debate over police brutality, police officers often explained to me that they feel trapped by competing pressures: their responsibility or duty to protect, the (perceived) danger they face themselves in the line of work, and the risk of prosecution and public condemnation. They told me that they feel as if they work "under a microscope," that any "small misstep" could have serious implications for both their professional careers and personal lives—even though few police officers who violate civil rights end up being prosecuted, let alone convicted. At the same time, police officers frequently stressed that they are part of society, that "there shouldn't be a distinction between the public and the police department," as one commanding officer argued. "I also live in a neighborhood where I feel responsible for safety: I want the same as they do." In light of threats made against the police on social media as well as actual coverage of violence against police officers, some officers expressed their support for Blue Lives Matter, a countermovement to Black Lives Matter (BLM). Founded after two officers were shot and killed in New York City in 2014, Blue Lives Matter argues that police officers are at risk throughout the United States and are often targeted by the public, though the number of police officers killed on duty is actually in decline (White et al. 2019). During one "roll call"—a meeting in which a sergeant provides updates to officers before they go out on patrol—the MPD sergeant shared a printed screenshot of a social media post, which claimed that the "Black Lives Matter movement did a radio broadcast telling their supporters/followers to kill any cops they see working alone on Friday September 11th." The author recommended readers to "spread the word to all your supervisors and cops to be extremely vigilant and cognizant of their surroundings."

This book aims to take our understanding of policing and police brutality beyond what might be encountered in the news and popular culture as "Black" versus "Blue" lives, showing both residents' and police officers' negotiations on behalf of safety and security. I want to emphasize that this does not mean that the implications of these everyday insecurities are in any way the same. On the contrary, whereas police officers act with a high level of impunity and a broad sense of righteousness, as well as widespread political endorsement and increased financial support, Black, Latinx, and other marginalized communities experience policing as a public health issue, that is, as a threat to their well-being. In general, governmental policies differentiate between racial groups by privileging the position of some while oppressing others. And in that vein, policing policies have conspicuously exacerbated inequalities among citizens based on race, gender, and class (see, e.g., Gordon 2019). Disenfranchised residents understand police incursions into their neighborhoods as threatening—not only because of the way the police behave and criminalize residents of these neighborhoods but also because the police are well funded and omnipresent. It is the main public agency persistently present in residents' lives and neighborhoods.

Yet the idea of the vigilant citizen also speaks to how the police as a racialized and violent institution has created contradictions and dangers for individual officers, who are themselves expected to figure out how to keep sane and safe in their daily work. To recognize these perceptions and experiences of police insecurity is not to support often highly problematic, if not illegal, police practices. Rather, as Kevin G. Karpiak and William Garriott write, it is "about acknowledging fallibility and other traits that are just as essential to what makes police—as both individuals and as an institution—human" (2018: 6). In other words, police officers feel that they are doing the right thing when they protect and defend themselves, making sure that "at the end of the day everybody goes home"—a statement painted on the white concrete walls of the MBPD parking garage, and thus the last thing that police officers see before they drive their patrol cars onto the streets of Miami Beach. This statement illustrates that police officers, too, are concerned about their own safety and are reminded that they are *citizens*, "people with families," who take off their uniform when their shift is over.

Explaining how these perceptions of insecurity and individual responsibility reproduce existing inequalities, I situate the workings of vigilant citizenship within the lived experiences of police brutality and racial injustice in and beyond the United States. Approximately a thousand people are killed by the police in the United States annually (Tate, Jenkins, and Rich 2022). A growing body of scholarship emphasizes that policing, and especially police gun violence, is rooted in the history of slave patrols. Connecting multiple racialized inequalities in both policing and criminal justice, Laurence Ralph (2019), for instance, shows "what Black people have been alleging for centuries: African Americans are policed and punished far more severely than their white counterparts" (2019: 2). This fact has only become more evident in recent footage showing police officers resorting to disproportionate and often lethal violence against Black citizens.

Racial disparities in policing, however, extend beyond antagonistic relationships and violent encounters between Black residents and police officers, that is, "well beyond the bounds of institutions and interactions traditionally understood as 'police'" (Karpiak and Garriott 2018: 4). In the context of neoliberal policies, state agencies have shifted the responsibility for protecting body and property on to citizens. In Miami, state agencies encourage residents to make their own security measures, to share information about crime with authorities, and to mobilize various weapons and technologies in order to keep themselves safe. Increasingly, a diverse range of actors, from the police to neighborhood-watch groups to private security companies, is involved in policing. In Florida, the most infamous example in recent years was the case of George Zimmerman, a neighborhood-watch captain who shot and killed Trayvon Martin, an unarmed Black teenager, in 2012. Zimmerman was eventually acquitted of all charges, on the basis that his actions constituted a form of self-defense justified under Florida's stand-your-ground legislation. It is no surprise that civil rights activists based in Miami specifically use

Figure I.2. The names Demz, Reefa, Trayvon Martin, and M. Brown on a mural tombstone in Wynwood, April 2015.

the term "deputized citizens" to talk about the ways in which people in general are increasingly endowed with the legal right to use lethal force. They emphasize that in practice, policing actors—not only the police but also neighborhood-watch members such as Zimmerman—often fail to protect vulnerable citizens and are sources of danger and insecurity themselves. In their view, this has sustained a culture in which violence against Black residents continues to be acceptable and legalized. More recent examples of "deputized citizens" include the murder of Ahmaud Arbery by three white men in Georgia in 2020, and the case of Kyle Rittenhouse, who shot three and killed two unarmed citizens during a BLM demonstration in Kenosha, Wisconsin, also in 2020.

Dream Defenders, the local branch of the BLM movement in Miami, was largely organized around police brutality and racial injustice. After the lack of indictments in the police killings of Michael Brown in Ferguson and Eric Garner in New York in 2014, Dream Defenders organized a protest on the I-95 highway, blocking traffic in both directions after the busy Art Basel art fair. During these protests, the crowd used slogans such as "I can't breathe" and "Shut it down," by then well-known expressions used by movements against police brutality and state-sanctioned violence throughout the United States. In addition to Garner and Brown, protesters also referred to local cases, such as the deaths of Israel "Reefa"

Hernandez and Delbert "Demz" Rodriguez, two graffiti artists who died at the hands of police officers in Miami Beach and the neighborhood of Wynwood, respectively. A painted tombstone on one of Wynwood's murals, displaying together the names of Trayvon Martin, Michael Brown, Demz, and Reefa, is a key illustration of the insertion of Miami into the national narrative and vice versa (see figure 1.2). These combined references exemplify how police brutality is interpreted through a broader experience of racialized violence and injustice, in which victims of public and private policing actors are united in their memorialization.

My analysis of vigilant citizenship seems especially relevant in light of global neoliberal norms, in particular the increasing involvement of citizens in violent and extralegal acts. I highlight similarities in terms of how state agencies have used citizenship to mobilize citizens for policing purposes in cities across the world, and how state agencies have framed societal issues such as insecurity and inequality as problems of personal choice and agency. These connections do not signify the devolution of public-security responsibilities on to the private sector: neoliberalism leads to a rapid growth of the carceral state and the use of the penal system, resulting in extreme policing practices and mass imprisonment (Wacquant 2001). What stands out, in other words, is neither a decline of state involvement nor exhaustive shifts in terms of responsibility for security provision, but, rather, the increase in the number of people who believe and act as if they are individually responsible for their personal safety. Focusing on broader experiences of self-defense and the cultivation of distrust and fear, I draw on the case of the vigilant citizen to show how policing in and beyond the state—across institutions, actors, and settings—perpetuates and intensifies urban inequalities. The vigilant ideal, in other words, speaks to a form of self-protection and self-regulation in which citizens live up to safety standards as well as self-regulated legal and ethical codes.

This independent and individualistic ideal of self-reliance is not only centered on violence; it also involves a particularly masculine approach to citizenship. While the ethnographic stories in this book focus on the importance of racial difference in Miami, especially for policing, they also tend to be masculinist (including my own perspective): many respondents identify as male, and most urban sites are highly gendered spaces that also skew male. Recognizing this intersectionality allows for discussions of how the vigilant citizen is emplaced, embodied, and materialized, compelling us to recognize how policing also produces and reflects gendered practices and experiences. Together, the individualization of responsibility and the "rational" and gendered practices of self-protection lie at the core of what we have come to understand and experience as vigilant citizenship in the twenty-first-century city.

Everyday Policing

As Stuart Hall noted in the late 1970s, policing involves institutionalized practices and responses to perceived threats through which a social order is established and maintained. Highly racialized imaginaries of crime and danger provide the "basis for the justification of extreme reaction[s] (social, judicial, political) to the crime problem" (Hall et al. 1978: 26). Despite police reforms and attempts to increase transparency and accountability, racialized police brutality remains an everyday reality for poor and Black citizens. More recently, scholars point out how the work of the police has always been about the use of violence. Micol Seigel (2018), for instance, suggests thinking of police officers as "violence workers": they instantiate the core power of the state and its perceived monopoly on the use of force. Critical of narratives of the police that romanticize its origins, and the contemporary "idea of the police" (e.g., Bittner 1970; Júnior and Muniz 2006) as an intrinsically benevolent and professional institution, Seigel shows how policing is rooted in racism and violence, and legitimized through perceptions and experiences of crime.

Nevertheless, law enforcement agencies in the United States have long successfully defended themselves against accusations and visual testimonies of police brutality. By pointing the finger at individual officers, a wide range of actors, from police departments to US presidents, continues to invoke the so-called bad-apple explanation (e.g., Punch 2003), suggesting that only a few officers use exceptional violence, and that this is mainly a problem of character and personal decision-making that can be addressed at the individual level.[5] Such explanations intersect with the ideal of vigilant citizenship and neglect what Kevin F. Steinmetz and colleagues call the "colonial character of contemporary American policing" (2016: 69). This is not to imply that policing today is the same as during colonial times, but rather that its current racialized order, especially in the American "ghetto," is simply a modern extension of colonial logics and oppression. The American racial caste system, built on Jim Crow laws that legalized and institutionalized racial segregation, never disappeared but has been merely "redesigned" (Alexander 2012). And as an iconic and extremely well-funded governmental agency, the police still very much stand at the forefront of this system, as illustrated by the school-to-prison pipeline, the prison-industrial complex, and the racialized realities of intrusive and violent policing practices in everyday life.

It is important to recognize that racialized antagonism and violence are also visible in various forms of nonstate policing. Scholarship has concentrated on formal and informal constellations of policing actors and security practices. Indeed, the commodification, privatization, and pluralization of policing have been central themes across academic disciplines, and scholars have produced several concepts to capture the daily realities of policing and inequality, including "security assemblages" (Abrahamsen and Williams 2011), "local security networks" (Dupont 2004), and "twilight policing" (Diphoorn 2015). These studies have predominantly focused on the relationships between security providers, state actors, and residential communities, and they have explored the development and the causalities of the proliferation of policing actors in everyday life.

Other theorizations of policing have explicitly sought to incorporate the phenomenon of citizen responsibility. Hayal Akarsu (2020), for instance, discusses how the Turkish National Police has invested heavily in community policing to curtail systemic police brutality. Akarsu demonstrates, however, how such attempts have led to what she calls "citizen forces": a kind of ancillary police force in which citizens actually "help consolidate state power and aggravate state repression, especially against suspect Others" (2020: 27). Similarly, Andrew Newman (2012) uses the term *vigilant citizenship* to conceptualize how state agencies mobilize residents of lower-income neighborhoods in Paris for the purpose of having them monitor and control one another under the guise of "civic engagement." Sean P. Hier and Josh Greenberg (2012) refer to several government policies that promote the responsibility of citizens to arrange for their own security. In addition, and directly related to the geographical context of this book, consider Jennifer Carlson's (2015) work on private gun ownership and the notion of "citizen-protectors" in the United States. Carlson shows how guns "work to address real and imagined social, economic, and physical insecurities" (2015: 9). Exploring "a world in which guns are attractive not only to white men but also to racial minorities" (2015: 9), Carlson explains how guns become meaningful in the hands of many, and how a "politics of gun carry stipulates new moral codes for how a responsible citizen should behave in a context saturated with socioeconomic insecurity and aggravated by the state's failure to adequately provide security" (2015: 10).

Similarly, my own research in Miami shows how state agencies have shifted the responsibility for protecting body and property on to citizens. Moving beyond more traditional approaches in criminology and policing studies, which tend to focus on the workings and experiences of a particular policing actor, I aim to advance understanding of the myriad ways policing produces and perpetuates inequality and injustice. This means that my aim in this book is not merely to emphasize the proliferation of actors involved in everyday policing and the reproduction of a racialized social order. Rather, I trouble binary divisions between policing actors and citizens involved in policing and emphasize the similarities in their experiences of safety and insecurity. In Miami, police officers work for private businesses, public agencies hire private security guards, and residents participate in neighborhood-watch groups to live up to ideals of self-defense. Through the lens of vigilant citizenship, I examine these relationships and interactions between public and private policing actors, but more important, I explain how vigilant citizenship engenders shifts in the roles these actors take on, and what this means for them in terms of safety and belonging.

Vigilant Citizenship

For those who are still wondering, there are no federal laws prohibiting police officers from carrying personal weapons such as knives while on duty. And if local departments do not enforce otherwise, police officers seem comfortable in doing so, and openly show them in front of other police officers and citizens. Does this make the MBPD officer a vigilant citizen? Instead of delineating who is and who is not a vigilant citizen, this book asks how people enact and experience vigilant citizenship:

What are the advantages, difficulties, and complexities of vigilant citizenship, especially when it is propagated by the government? And who benefits from vigilant citizenship?

Following others with ethnographic and practice-based approaches, this book examines how vigilant citizenship informs everyday acts and experiences of policing (e.g., Isin 2008; Lazar 2008). This approach is especially relevant considering the increasing involvement and individual responsibility of residents in violent and extralegal acts. Police shootings, riots, civil disobedience, lynching, and other forms of vigilantism can all be understood as ways in which ordinary people define and express different sorts of belonging and rights (see Goldstein 2010; Risør 2010). While vigilant citizenship helps to legitimize the lethal actions of the likes of Zimmerman, it also informs daily acts and more mundane interactions that underlie physical violence against racialized others. In the next chapter, I show how constantly watching your neighbors and neighborhood, keeping an eye out for anything "suspicious," is a key part of what it means to be a vigilant citizen. In chapter 2, I discuss how carrying a gun at a time and in a place where this is not legal could still be considered an act and experience of vigilant citizenship. A private security guard who keeps the gun on his ankle a secret at work believes that the circumstances in which he would use the gun would also legitimize his decision to carry a concealed weapon in the first place. And as I explain in chapter 3, many consider owning, carrying, and using a weapon to be a fundamental aspect of what it means to be a vigilant citizen.

Vigilant citizenship is a distinct elaboration of a citizenship agenda, "a normative framing of citizenship that prescribe[s] what norms, values, and behavior are appropriate for those claiming membership of a political community" (de Koning et al. 2015: 121). In this case, this normativity is informed by neoliberal ideologies and policies in which citizens are imagined as rational subjects capable of navigating assets and liabilities of their own accord, and therefore individually liable for insecurity, misconduct, and illegal violence. While my use of *vigilant citizen* includes references to the popular mindset of awareness (*vigilance*) and extralegal actions meant to improve feelings of safety and justice (*vigilantism*), I specifically mobilize the concept to refer to the institutionalization and normalization of practices of watchful self-protection. Here, I foreground an analysis of "self-policing": a form of self-regulation in which individuals monitor their own adherence to legal, ethical, and safety standards. "Responsibility," as Susanna Trnka and Catherine Trundle argue, "becomes a form of reflexive prudence, and individuals and collectives must increasingly conduct evaluations of their actions in relation to their potential effects, calculating and designing their life course in ways that attempt to mitigate harm and risk, and maximize benefit to themselves and others" (2014: 139).

As to the implications of vigilant citizenship for everyday policing, three main attitudes can be identified: a heightened level of awareness and watchfulness, the willingness to own and use a gun, and the tendency to recontextualize violent policing practices through a legal lens. First, states have mobilized citizens for a range of security-related concerns, attuned to the search for suspicious activities and the reporting of these activities to the police. Such interpersonal or peer-monitoring forms of surveillance are called "lateral surveillance." Through such policies and efforts, state agencies aim to create vigilant citizens who act in line with an identity at once individual and national, that fragments feelings of collectivity rather than supports projects of shared belonging. Second, guns are a core element of security in Miami and a central premise of various articulations of vigilant citizenship. Although estimates vary, Florida's gun-ownership percentage is around 35, and the state has the highest percentage of concealed-carry permits in the United States (over two million out of a total population of twenty-one million).[6] Vigilant citizens understand gun ownership as not only a right but also an essential duty and responsibility in terms of personal safety. Yet vigilant citizenship's individualized logic of self-protection and defense emphasized by vigilant citizenship obscures the interdependencies between private gun ownership, state-sanctioned violence, and white supremacy. Finally, vigilant citizenship influences responses to policing, most notably the widespread use of cameras, especially cell phone cameras. Although cameras can be effectively used to visualize and document civil rights abuses in everyday life, there is also a strong tendency to understand recordings of police brutality in terms of legal culpability and individual liability. Such a juridical way of interpreting systemic violence and institutionalized racism is directly related to vigilant citizenship, as it recontextualizes the violent and racialized nature of policing in terms of self-protection and accountability. Working across these themes, this book analyzes how vigilant citizenship frames abusive policing as an experience of individual misconduct and traces the cascading effects of structural inequality and racial injustice in everyday life in Miami.

Imagining Miami

Miami is the name for a metropole in South Florida with 2.7 million residents that consists of several different cities, including the cities of Miami and Miami Beach, each with its own police department. In terms of demography, the population of Miami is considered to be "diverse," with 69.4% Latinx, 17.7% Black, and 12.9% non-Hispanic white residents.[7] Miami is characterized by the influx of migrants and refugees who have settled in the metropolitan area during the past few decades. As a relatively secure and politically stable area of the United States, Miami is imagined as conducive to social mobility, and it has continued to attract migrants at every stage of its relatively short history. In particular, Miami has long been a destination of choice for Cubans who have been migrating to the city since the late nineteenth century. Since 1980, when 125,000 Cubans and 40,000 Haitians arrived in Miami in the span of one year, most of them as refugees, the number of residents with a Latin American background has increased considerably. The Latinx population eventually became the majority, and Spanish became a language of everyday life alongside English.

Most researchers who study Miami therefore focus on how these migrant population groups, especially Cuban Americans, have transformed the urban environment. Alejandro Portes and Ariel C. Armony observe that "if non-Hispanic whites represent the 'mainstream' of the American population, then that mainstream had disappeared in Miami" (2018: 23). Scholars have dubbed Miami the "capital of Latin America" (Portes and Stepick 1993) and the "gateway to the Americas" (Nijman 2011). Focusing on its geographical position and resident migrant groups, they point out that Miami offers unique business opportunities. In their view, companies based in Miami can tap into Latin American markets while enjoying the regulatory protections and legal environment of the United States. In *City on the Edge*, Alejandro Portes and Alex Stepick argue that "Miami is not a microcosm of the American city. It never was" (1993: xi).

Based on its rapid growth through emigration from Spanish-speaking nations, they depict Miami as a melting pot with a fundamentally different sociopolitical and cultural character than that of other US cities.

These scholarly framings have also favored an understanding of Miami as a transnational gateway and exceptional city within the United States. "Imagining Miami," the title for this section, echoes Sheila Croucher's (1997) work on ethnic politics in Miami. Croucher argues that ethnic ties and tensions in the city are not merely the result of Miami's social, political, and economic change but also an integral part of such. For example, she shows how the popular idea of the Cuban success story presents Cubans as white, hardworking individuals who deserve their success, in contrast with African Americans who do not. She notes that "tales of individual freedom and enterprise, or in other words, fulfilling the American Dream, influence the construction of social realities that are rooted in power and politics" (1997: 141).

In *A World More Concrete*, a history of real estate and racial segregation in South Florida, Nathan B. Connolly (2014) explains how racial apartheid became a sociopolitical, especially spatio-material, reality in Miami. Local residents, scholars, and journalists often depict Miami's rapid growth since its establishment in 1896 as magical, indicating a sense of disbelief at how fast Miami was apparently constructed out of thin air, from the wilderness into a fully developed city. In less than six months, Miami had a newspaper, a bank, and several stores and churches. Writing about South Florida's early development, Grunwald (2006) states that "nothing was crazier than the real estate market" and that "Miami was epicenter of the insanity" (2006: 177, 179). Miami's "magic" was built and made possible by mostly Black work crews, who constructed a railway track from North to South Florida (Jacksonville to Key West) for the oil tycoon Henry Flagler's railway company. In Flagler's view, railway track was essential to burnishing Miami's reputation in business circles, which would—and indeed did—translate into the city's rapid development (Connolly 2014). Because of the rising demand for cheap labor, the Caribbean American and African American populations kept growing. In Miami's early years, these groups made up 40 percent of the city's total population. While white residents relied on them to build the city's infrastructure, they also protested the expansion of the Black population. Flagler eventually helped establish "Colored

Town," a specifically designed area for the city's growing Black labor force (Connolly 2014; Nijman 2011). This area eventually became known as Overtown.

In his account of Miami, Connolly (2014) does not tell a story of exceptional people enduring exceptional hardships in an exceptional place. Rather, as he puts it, Connolly "has offered a regrettably commonplace and *un*exceptional story about how people sought and used power over the land to make and unmake wealth, neighborhoods, and individual and collective identities" (2014: 278; original emphasis). Despite its "glittering reputation and its tremendous cultural and linguistic diversity, Greater Miami was nothing special. It remained as economically dependent on a white-over-black system as more industrialized US cities, such as Birmingham, Alabama, or Chicago" (Connolly 2014: 6).

The case of Miami has also helped some scholars to understand urban apartheid in the United States as variation on a theme, namely, that of colonialism as seen in other parts of the world (e.g., Nightingale 2012; Connolly 2014; Gosin 2019). Miami's very visible inequality and racial segregation, as well as its more concealed power structures, are expressions of national and international systems of exploitation and white supremacy. In Miami-Dade, the county in which Miami sits, there are vast disparities between Black Miamians and their Hispanic and white counterparts in terms of income, schooling, home ownership, and employment. In 2018, the median income for Black households was $18,512 lower than that for households identifying as white. Around 25 percent of Miami's Black population is officially impoverished, compared with the countywide rate of 16 percent.[8]

As it is a strongly divided and segregated city, numerous TV shows, videogames, and movies—including *Miami Vice*, *CSI: Miami*, *Dexter*, *Grand Theft Auto: Vice City*, and *Scarface*—have used Miami as a chic yet gritty setting, a vice-ridden city marked by glamour, crime, and insecurity. In his hit song "Hustlin'" (2006), Miami rapper Rick Ross explains that the city's reputation as a "playboy paradise" is "just a facade: the bridge separates South Beach from my Miami, the real Miami." In the corresponding music video, we see Ross driving a white BMW across the bridge, leaving Miami Beach to enter that part of Miami where mostly Black and Latinx residents live and work: the place where he "hustles." In her work on the effects of civic culture on public policy,

Juliet Gainsborough suggests that "any discussion of Miami is really a discussion about two different Miamis" (2008: 419); she views Miami as a city of socioeconomic extremes, without a significant middle class. Quantitative studies (e.g., Bloomberg 2016) support the perception of Miami as a highly unequal city, consistently ranking the metropole as one of the poorest cities in the United States, even as it houses some of the wealthiest residential enclaves in the nation.

Popular culture, city marketing, and official crime records during the Miami drug wars of the 1980s gave the city an international reputation for crime. In 1987, a *New York Times* article asked whether Miami, a city "beset by drugs and violence," could still save itself from organized crime. It did. According to the City of Miami's police department, current crime rates are at a historic low, with fifty-one homicides in 2018, the lowest since 1967 (Rabin 2019). City officials attribute this decrease to police practices such as mounted police patrols, more surveillance cameras, and community policing. In the *Miami Herald*, Miami's main newspaper, Miami Police Chief Jorge Colina commented in 2019 on how the relationship between the police and residents of specific neighborhoods has improved: "people call us now to say where there are guns stashed. That wasn't happening before."[9] While crime rates in Miami have dropped since the 1980s, as in many other US cities, there is still a tendency for politicians and security professionals to "act as if we're still living under drug-crisis conditions."[10] Echoing this sentiment, local residents sometimes refer to Miami as a "sunny city with shady people," reflecting widespread feelings of insecurity, suspicion, and distrust. Sensationalistic stories, such as the case of the "Miami zombie," where a man bit off a large part of the face of another man sleeping under a causeway in 2012, also feed into Miami's image as an insecure and unpredictable urban environment in which a fear of Black crime plays a central role (Linnemann et al. 2014).

Like many other cities in the United States, Miami has seen several periods of intense political protest. In general, these protests have revolved around police brutality, ethnic and racial tensions, and the criminalization of neighborhoods in Miami such as Overtown, Opa Locka, and Liberty City. Between 1980 and 1990, four major riots occurred in Miami, the first following the acquittal of four Miami-Dade police officers over the killing of Arthur McDuffie in 1979. McDuffie died from injuries sustained at the hands of four white officers, who sought to arrest the salesman after a car chase (Croucher 1997). During these "McDuffie riots," police and military forces installed a curfew and used blockades and sniper fire to disperse the crowds, ending the riots after three days, and killing eighteen and injuring hundreds in the process. In 2015, a local resident discovered that the North Miami Beach Police had used images of Black men for target practice. She recognized her brother's mug shot at a shooting range, as one of several pictures at which the officers had been firing. In response, the police chief apologized and prohibited the use of mug shots for future target practice. Nevertheless, the case exemplifies the institutionalized racialization of policing in Miami, which requires public exposure before the authorities will even consider dealing with it. In the above example, the police department stopped using the mug shots for target practice only after the *Miami Herald* had written about it (Savransky 2015). The chief of police told the press that he felt really bad about the matter, but he refused to enter into dialogue with BLM activists who had called for his resignation.

A "European" Ethnography of Policing

My brief interaction with the Officer Hernandez in the book's opening story is indicative of the relationships I developed with Miami's police officers and other respondents during my fieldwork. Because of my "European" background, some police officers were more willing to explain their perspectives to me and were more forgiving of my "different" interpretation of security and police work. Many officers appeared open to the idea of having a researcher present, watching and talking to them during their work, and some even tried to involve me in their interactions with local residents. While I remained open about my work as a graduate student and researcher, officers still misunderstood my role and thought that I was learning to become a police officer myself. This gave me the impression that my access to the police as a civilian, as well as a non-US citizen, was quite unusual. Nevertheless, I participated in classes with recruits, interviewed commanding officers, observed community policing projects in various neighborhoods and homeless outreach programs, trained for SWAT swimming courses in a "heavy suit," visited holding cells, joined meetings with local residents, observed small-scale drug dealing on a corner while hiding in the bushes across the street, and participated in other aspects of police and civilian training such as crime-scene investigation. Other officers considered my views naive and saw Europeans as mostly a "bunch of liberals" who did not understand the daily reality of policing, especially not in the United States, let alone Miami. Yet this was exactly why I had come to Miami in the first place: to examine everyday policing in an American city characterized by urban inequality and police brutality, from the perspective of both policing actors and those being policed.

Many people, both in the United States and in the Netherlands, wondered why I had gone to research Miami in the first place, asking what "we" could possibly learn from my work. Such comments exemplify the politics of global knowledge production, in which few European researchers conduct qualitative research in the United States. Realizing that there is already a tendency in the Netherlands to see American life through stereotypes, which offers a limited understanding of policing and "trigger-happy" citizens, I often struggled with the presentation of my research findings in lectures and writing, both academic and public. I did not want to explain inequalities and violence as a cultural phenomenon, overlooking that policing practices across the world are rooted in European expansion and colonialization. I realize that opening this book with the anecdote of a police officer who carries three knives in holsters marked with Christian symbols does not help to deconstruct such stereotypes. Yet such examples can also be meaningful to foreground shared practices, beliefs, and ideologies in which racism and individual responsibility are key and indicative of a global system of white power (Beliso-De Jesús and Pierre 2020). In doing so, I connect my ethnographic findings of everyday policing—accounts of various security practices, institutional policies, and lived experiences—to broader conditions of urban inequality and racialized injustice.

While certain forms of violence and individualism, including private gun ownership, are perhaps not as common and valued in the Netherlands as in the United States, such limited framings neglect the socioeconomic factors and racialized politics that shape the way policing is enacted and experienced in the first place. In other words, though official statistics might suggest that the police are not as aggressive or lethal in the Netherland they do not say much about institutionalized racism and the lived experiences of ethnic profiling and violence more generally: police brutality is about much more than police killings. Police discrimination and hostility toward migrants in the Netherlands is widespread and effectively legitimized through bureaucratic and legal practices, and politics and populism continue to shape police work (Mutsaers 2019). Likewise, activists I spoke to in Miami were often critical of the broader European approach to institutionalized racism and policing. Philip Agnew, cofounder of Dream Defenders, taught me that the antiracism movement in the United States is far more advanced and organized compared with that in Europe, where even the talk of racism in public debate is still often avoided and considered irrelevant.

My aim to speak to larger debates of policing and urban inequality in the United States, however, has clear implications for gauging how representative the experiences of the people I talk about in this book are. This book features the perspectives and experiences of some of the city's many Latin American residents, including police officers, and offers insight into the relations of power between various population groups in Miami. Yet I aim to focus also on the sociopolitical status and experiences of African American and Haitian American residents, in ways that go beyond a focus on Black Miamians as the perpetrators and victims of street crime, "real-life" and fictional. Working across diverse neighborhoods and residents, the stories of Latinx experiences I tell in this book remain secondary to the self-perceptions of the Black community. While this might be surprising given that Miami is 60 percent Latinx, I found that the dynamics of Black criminalization were particularly salient and more indicative of national trends and conditions. As Raymond A. Mohl suggested long ago, the history of Black Miami has generally played second fiddle to Miami's stories of Latin American migration and the American Dream: "Black Miami was shuffled off into the shadows" (1989: 66). This has not changed in recent academic research.

My appearance as a white European man also affected my relationships with key interlocutors from these communities. Some, including police officers and security guards, appeared to feel more comfortable in disclosing their prejudices about, and displeasures with, Black residents to me. It was difficult for me to find a balance between distancing myself from their statements and stigmatizing beliefs, on the one hand, and maintaining a good working relationship with them, on the other. Indeed, I often found myself studying what Susan Harding (1991) calls "the repugnant cultural other." These "others," whom scholars often critique, if not despise, include elites, capitalists, white people, the military—and the police. Grace Carey (2019) explains how these people are often collectively dehumanized and what we must do to refrain from "painting pictures of homogeneity amongst group members and reifying modern subjectivities." As Carey points out, it is important to humanize these actors, not only to destabilize "us" and "them" categories but also to "build better politics and political action." By researching policing through the lens of citizenship—focused on how policing actors make sense of their rights, responsibilities, and belonging, and paying attention to the everyday worlds of police officers and blatantly racist white residents—I was (at times) better able to break down such binaries in policing.

My appearance, of course, also shaped my interactions with Black Miamians. My presence not only stood out, as I explained earlier, it also interfered with how my relationships with these residents developed. Luz, an African American MPD police officer in her early thirties, for example, told me that she wanted to go to law school. I asked if she wanted to use the degree to return to the MPD afterward, perhaps to apply for a higher-ranking position. She was careful when formulating her answer: "I don't want to offend you but . . . I think that would be for more lighter skinned people." Her words surprised me. I had been meeting with Luz on a more or less weekly basis for some ten months, and I had assumed she understood my interest in understanding and critiquing racism. Yet she did not feel comfortable expressing her concerns and beliefs to me. I reassured her there was no way she could offend me by saying something like that, yet the interaction illustrated how difficult it was to develop relationships with my respondents in which racial inequalities could be discussed openly. Perhaps unsurprising, these interlocutors appeared to be much more willing to discuss these issues with nonwhite residents or visitors (including a colleague of mine) who share similar experiences and backgrounds.

I moved around Miami by bike and sometimes by car. Modes of transportation in the city are strongly intertwined with class: pedestrians, cyclists, and those who rely on the city's cumbersome public transport system are generally of a lower socioeconomic background than those who can afford to use a car. Miami's car-based infrastructure and layout limit the mobility of those without one. While a bike proved essential to meet people and discover new places, it also raised eyebrows. Who was this white man on a bike? Police officers explained to me that whenever they saw a white man in the streets of Overtown, they generally assumed he was there to buy and consume illegal drugs. They told me that there was a high likelihood that the police would stop me—though this never happened. Some local residents also sought to point me in the right direction of where to buy such substances, and they explained to me that I was safe in Overtown precisely because I was white. Two hairdressers in Overtown said I was seen as a potential and valuable customer, and that drug dealers would look to protect any buyers in the neighborhood. While in practice my actual behavior might have countered such assumptions, my presence in all neighborhoods, but particularly in Overtown, was highly noticeable to both residents and visitors.

Although I always introduced myself as a graduate student, many residents were unfamiliar with qualitative research and occasionally some became suspicious of who I was and why I was asking certain questions. My name, appearance (as a tall white man), and research interests combined to make it difficult for some to categorize me and assess my integrity. I stood out in most settings. Except for when I was with Olaf, my white roommate with a somewhat similar sartorial style and height, I always felt out of place in Miami. One reason for this was because my appearance was generally not as "styled" or "clean" as that of many other Miamians. This was partly due to my work as an ethnographer, which required me to be outside, often on foot in the heat or on my bike. The respondents I would meet or interview, in contrast, often worked inside, and wore business attire or fashionable pants and shirts, while I arrived in shorts. There were several people who jokingly commented on this, and though it made me feel uncomfortable at times, it seemed to also balance the "serious" scope and aim of my research and make my respondents more willing to discuss controversial issues.

Throughout my fieldwork, I had to navigate relationships of authority and trust, and there were of course times that police officers were uncomfortable with my presence. Didier Fassin translates a quote by Christian Mouhanna (2007), a French sociologist, who argues that "any scrutiny or critical gaze based on in-depth knowledge of police circles represents a danger. Clearly, if the policy in force essentially aims not at modifying police practices but at improving the image of law enforcement bodies, the slightest divergence in analysis is likely to disturb the authorities" (2013: 17). Fassin understands the sensitivity of this knowledge in a twofold manner: as a key reason behind police departments' unwillingness to accept the involvement of external researchers and journalists, especially in volatile times; and as an explanation for the difficulties he experienced in establishing a working relationship with police departments in France. Miami police officers were also suspicious of an external gaze, of someone quite literally looking over their shoulders as they worked. Although the officers whom I got acquainted with often saw me as a student—one perhaps a bit annoying but not a threat to their integrity—others who were not familiar with my work were sometimes less comfortable with my presence. In one instance, I was observing a training class when a police instructor explained to his class that "the media is doing us absolutely no favors." Soon after, I was told I was no longer able to continue observing his class.

It is understandable that the presence of a researcher causes anxiety, regardless of one's profession. You do not have to be a police officer to find it annoying or disconcerting when somebody asks questions about your work. However, I found that there was also a second factor that shaped my access to the two police departments: legal liability. Both the MBPD and MPD set a fixed number of times that I was allowed to accompany a patrol officer on duty. Their concern with liability did not automatically translate to measures directed at enhancing my personal safety, as I was never required to wear body armor, though the officers I accompanied sometimes did. Officers told me that they expected my relatives to sue the police department should I sustain injuries during a patrol shift. This, they believed, was why I had been given a limited number of hours, why I had to sign disclaimers and waivers before every shift, and why the community-relations sergeant had to check my background for criminal offenses every single time I wanted to accompany a patrol officer. Nevertheless, my research took place at a time when police departments were looking to "reinvent themselves," as Daniel Oates, chief of the MBPD, told me. This meant that they were looking for a proper balance between transparency and the protection of sensitive information and police practices. I managed to benefit from this development, as I gained access to most of the MPD's and MBPD's main activities during my research.

While it was understandable that not everyone would be willing to discuss sensitive issues with a relative stranger like myself, a strong legal culture and suspiciousness seemed to play a larger role in shaping my interlocutors' responses. People were careful when engaging in certain debates and in verbalizing their answers. I was told that there were many private detectives in Miami, and that they did exactly what I was doing: asking questions. It took Alfredo, a graduate student, local resident, and good friend, six months to acquire the telephone number of one of his key respondents. Even though my appearance and position as a student allowed me to affiliate myself with various actors during my fieldwork, it took time and patience to explain my research and build relationships. Yet despite the politically volatile times, and the increased scrutiny of police practices across the country, there seemed to be little hesitation to pair me with officers who had a reputation among their colleagues for being aggressive; a reputation that sometimes became apparent as I observed their interactions with residents.

Both within and without their working environments, I spoke with police officers about their professional and private lives. I listened to officers discuss how they had dealt with issues they encountered in their work, and I greeted recruits who saluted me in the morning as I came to visit their class. I also noted conversations and interactions between police officers, as eventually I was able to move with relative freedom within the MPD. I spent time with police instructors during lunches at the police station and during training sessions, and frequently interacted with policing actors in the different neighborhoods. I attended public events and protests where local residents encountered police officers and spoke to all of them. Some police officers showed me where they lived and where they worked "off duty," and talked about their future career plans as a law enforcement officer. While I was always honest about my research intentions, I did not necessarily convey all my opinions.

In addition to navigating access and authority within the police departments, a main concern during my fieldwork in Miami was that I was becoming increasingly involved with individuals and groups who held antagonistic beliefs. Sometimes I recognized police officers whom I had joined during a patrol shift while I was attending antiracism protests. I often decided to approach them and be open about my activities as a researcher, and this did not seem to concern them. I also became affiliated with the Wynwood Business Improvement District (BID). I wore an official BID shirt and helped them conduct a small survey concerning the safety and overall satisfaction of visitors in Wynwood, and I talked to developers who were looking to expand their activities in the neighborhood. Yet I also interviewed activists and joined protesters who were seeking to actively resist gentrification in Wynwood. I met with African American hairdressers Marcus and Fenix both inside and outside their barbershop in Overtown, a locale that MPD police officer Luz would drive past in her police car and that I passed by while doing a tour of the neighborhood with thirty police recruits. I sat with Santos, a Cuban American security guard, at the entrance of the bar where residents of Overtown sometimes came to drink. All my key interlocutors were aware of my involvement in different neighborhoods and with different groups. I did, however, try to minimize being visibly associated with the police, especially when a patrol officer reprimanded residents in Overtown, a neighborhood through which I was going to bike the next day; the tinted windows of the police cars helped avoid some potentially awkward encounters.

I also contacted two private security companies and several neighborhood-watch and crime-watch groups. I talked to the owners of both companies, visited their offices and training facilities, and joined a troop of guards in training at a shooting range. These experiences were particularly useful for contextualizing my interactions with Santos, a security guard employed by Xecurity, a pseudonym for the main company featured in this book, which was active in South Beach and Wynwood. Still, I draw more heavily on my observations and interactions with Miami's police officers than on my experiences with private security companies. This is primarily because of the significance of police officers in everyday policing, primarily due to their additional rights and associated sociopolitical status. In Miami, only law enforcement officers such as the police can make arrests, and there are specific laws and policies supporting police practices. In comparison, security guards are often unarmed and only allowed to act within set, predefined boundaries. In both popular culture and daily work, many people do not take the presence of security guards too seriously, and some mockingly call them "rent-a-cops." Although they dress like police officers and act like police officers, they clearly are not. Most of the time, they are paid minimum wage, have no additional benefits, and are expected to work long and tiresome shifts that involve few to no clear goals other than to observe and call the police in case of an incident. While police officers are granted additional rights to use violence, security guards are not. Instead, Santos, the security guard, told me he had to rely on his "verbal judo" skills to make people leave his employer's premises.

My access to the police departments in Miami provided insight into what criminologists refer to as "police culture." Back in 1985, Robert Reiner identified several key characteristics of police culture associated with violence, including masculinity, individuality, and suspicion. While such cultural values do not necessarily dictate how police officers approach their work, "the key to unpacking [any] culture," Holly Campeau writes, "is to unveil when, where and how particular sets of cultural resources are put to work" (2015: 670). Other scholars have come up with typologies of police officers and police work. Types of the "police officer" include the professional, "whose judicious exercise of authority is fettered by myriad rules and regulations," and the vigilante, who seizes on "popular demands for swift justice" (Hirschfield and Simon 2010: 157). Exploring the workings of dominant cultural notions in police culture, especially the idealized "warrior" mentality of the police, criminologists have published extensively on police reform. Yet such attempts to make policing more inclusive and less violent, including community policing, have rarely succeed in addressing the workings of institutionalized racism. In fact, by reifying the racialized narrative of criminalization, community policing programs actually sustain and intensify police brutality and discrimination (Raschig 2018; Souhami 2012; Stoughton 2016). What remains is a need to understand everyday policing across different actors and beyond institutional cultures.

My work with the police raises questions of my own responsibility, legal and moral. To wit, what to do with observations or information that concerns violence or illegal activities? When asked, officers often introduced me as a "Dutch police student" or similar phrase during ride-alongs and interactions with residents. Indeed, I felt "awkward,"—as Gareth A. Jones and Dennis Rodgers (2019: 314) note, when they presented me as one of them and thus a "potential perpetrator of violence" (2019: 303), a role often overlooked in debates on participant-observation and ethnographic research more generally.

During the few moments I witnessed physical encounters and the use of force, I stood back and joined the ranks of other bystanders, where I often was the only one who did not use my cellphone to record police use of force. I remained silent after observing aggressive actions when I did not know what to say, or casually asked the police officers involved to reflect on what had just happened. I never left the scene, however. Much of my work with the police was a mixture of emotions, including excitement (when they raced through the city using sirens) and fear (when they drew their weapon or became anxious), and I often felt myself unable to objectively assess of what was happening, especially during intense and busy patrols.

Finally, given the sensitive nature of my research—working with antagonistic groups and discussing illegal activities—I struggled with how to protect the identities of my interlocutors and my own positionality. While I use pseudonyms throughout, I was unsure of how my position of power vis-à-vis the people I studied would affect their livelihoods, both during and after my fieldwork. Ethnographic research involves engaging "in deep relationships where trust is extremely important" (Grassiani 2020: 251). Yet these relationships are highly unequal. I did try to support them—I helped with logistics, contacts, and sometimes financial support. But this hardly makes it even. Over the course of this project, I grew increasingly uncomfortable with the part of my research that concerned studying subaltern groups. Still informed by classical anthropological notions of "giving people a voice," I felt that it was important to engage and represent the experience of Black Miamians. Yet skeptical of the idea that the empathy of a white foreign researcher is in any way beneficial to these groups, I foregrounded my work with the police and those on the other side of the power balance over more elaborate stories of African American residents and experiences. My focus on the police is also a way of studying power that I, as a Dutch white researcher, could access and hence critically engage. This role enables me to speak to issues of racism, violence, and inequality in ways that go beyond "giving others a voice" that has been long heard yet often purposefully ignored by those spotlighted in this book.

What Comes Next

The BLM movement, and those supportive of the cause, have continually risen up against racialized police brutality, both with and without visual testimonies of police killings, injustice, and violence. In spring 2020, people all over the world once again mobilized against institutionalized racism, particularly as evidenced in police departments. Activists, journalists, and scholars have increasingly begun to recognize the need for political and cultural change, joining community calls to defund and abolish the police, and agitating for inclusive forms of public safety. At the height of this movement, Derek Chauvin, the Minneapolis police officer who killed George Floyd, was found guilty and convicted of multiple charges, including second-degree unintentional murder. While constituting a remarkable exception to the rule, the conviction did not necessarily result in structural change, including the defunding of police departments and broader attempts in creating alternatives to modern policing. Examining widespread practices of self-defense and the cultivation of distrust and fear through the lens of vigilant citizenship, this book aims to contribute to progressive change by showing how such inequalities continue to be reproduced both in and beyond encounters with the police, and how they are recontextualized as the problems of citizens.

In the next chapter, "Places and Partnerships of Policing," I examine how everyday policing and the related socio-spatial inequality affect the experience of living and working in Miami. Through the perspectives of four key interlocutors in three neighborhoods, the chapter discusses how public and private actors work together in local security arrangements, how dominant perceptions of crime continue to affect the everyday lives of Black residents, how Black police officers understand their affiliations with police and nonpolice collectives, and how private security guards become part of intrusive policing practices. Together, these experiences outline everyday practices of class division, discrimination, and urban segregation in Miami and thereby provide the backdrop for the chapters to follow.

In chapter 2, "Do the Right Thing," I discuss how ideals of public vigilance campaigns and lateral surveillance programs have mobilized citizens for policing purposes, to have them surveil one another. Examining these programs and activities, this chapter aims to show how state agencies shape political subject formation at a local level. While there is nothing wrong with somebody calling the police to deal with individuals or groups who jeopardize public and private safety, lateral surveillance programs are much more likely to cultivate distrust, fear, and alienation, feeding into racialized and violent reactions by police officers and neighborhood-watch groups. State agencies articulate a citizenship agenda that emphasizes the contributions of a community of vigilant citizens to public safety—a community whose members contextualize situations and actions through racial categories that generate forms of privilege and disadvantage.

Tracing my experience with these communities and practices, chapter 3, "Guns for the Good Guys," examines the laws and practices surrounding private gun ownership. Unpacking the interdependencies of guns, policing, and race, this chapter shows how narratives of gun ownership create exclusive and racialized categories of "good" and "bad" guns. Guns, in other words, can have a different meaning and status depending on whose hands they are in. In addition, showing how gun ownership and use is embedded in notions of legality, and in ideals of law and order more broadly, this chapter aims to make clear that private gun ownership is an extension of state violence and racialized policing.

In chapter 4, "Looking through the Law," I delve deeper into how legality informs the way people interpret and evaluate policing practices. Focusing on the widespread use of body cameras and cell phones, I discuss how vigilant citizens tend to frame policing encounters in juridical terms. I found that police officers in particular tend to see and document their performances using visual "evidence." How police officers interact with citizens, and especially when they engage in violent and racist acts, is less about moral culpability, and more about legal culpability and specifically "legal-looking" performances. Police cameras thereby intensify existing notions of individual liability as a central aspect of vigilant citizenship, allowing an "incident" of police brutality to be decontextualized from the larger racist and violent ideologies that inform policing practices and protocol.

In the conclusion, titled "American Values?," I draw together these discussions to analyze how vigilant citizenship sustains, intensifies, and extends an intentional system of violence, racism, and insecurity.

This concluding chapter suggests that "being vigilant" enables an understanding of policing beyond police encounters. While the police remain a central actor in policing—both in this book and in everyday urban life in the United States—policing involves the mobilization of citizens, an emphasis on self-defense and vigilantism, and a state-backed legal system. I also point out how policing implies intimacy, increasingly affecting interpersonal relations, allegiances, and affectivities. Finally, I reflect on how my own understanding of Miami changed in the course of my research and the writing of this book. While this book aims to strengthen the critique of policing practices and actors, it does so by analyzing the lived realities of police officers, security guards, and armed citizens. It does so not to justify their practices and beliefs, but to emphasize how laws, norms, and policies continue to legitimize the involvement and actions of these violent actors in everyday life.

1

Places and Partnerships of Policing

It was 4 a.m. and Rico's uneventful shift was almost over. Only a few calls had come in. The MPD police officer parked his police car underneath a tree on a sidewalk in Wynwood, with the aim of spending the remaining hours there. It was around the time that most bars closed, and people would be driving home because few actually lived in the neighborhood and those who lived nearby tended to feel much safer driving than walking anyway. Hidden in the shadows, Rico had found a perfect spot to catch anyone running the red light at the intersection of NW Third Avenue and NW Twenty-Ninth Street. He had kept the car's engine running—to keep the air-conditioning working but also to respond immediately to any violations. When someone ignored the red light and passed directly in front of us, Rico switched on the police car's siren and advised me, "Hold on." I grabbed the roof handle with my

Figure 1.1. "Hire Overtown, End Segregation," March 2015.

right hand. The officer chased the car down, signaled the driver to pull over to the side of the road, gave her a ticket, and wished her a good and safe night. He returned to the hidden spot under the tree. This process repeated itself several times. In between these short chases, Rico talked about his experiences as a patrol officer working in different Miami neighborhoods. According to him, Overtown residents were particularly difficult for police officers to deal with. He explained that these residents "perceive they're targeted by us" and therefore "start talking about their rights whenever they see us, like we're the bad guys." Rico compared Overtown's African American residents with Latinx in Allapattah, an adjacent neighborhood. In his view, since many Latinx have experienced violent police practices in their countries of origin, "They have respect for law enforcement, because they have experience with a very corrupt police force. They learned not to talk back or to resist."

It was only a couple of hours earlier, however, that Rico himself had illustrated that it was not just the perception of Overtown residents that differed: they were actually policed differently. During his shift in the relatively small neighborhood, Rico drove slowly back and forth through the same streets, making last-minute and unexpected turns. Rico explained that he was "sharking": trying to catch people in the neighborhood off guard. "People think I'm driving one way," and he circled his finger in the air, "but then I come around." Rico was looking for cars that "make suspicious movements," such as backing up when they saw us parked at the end of the street. Rico recognized several residents in the neighborhood, often because he had arrested them before. Some of them started walking in the opposite direction and away from street corners when they noticed the police car we were in. He felt that everyone in Overtown "works together," and gave the example that people shout out "Nine!" whenever they see a police car coming through. Despite these perceived forms of social cohesion and collaboration, he still felt that he would be able to catch criminals in the act.

Rico's interpretation of Overtown as a high-crime area was a widely shared one. MPD officers had various ways to refer to specific parts of Overtown, including "the swamp" and "the hole," suggesting that it was some kind of urban jungle owned and run by those in the business of dealing drugs and peopled by those who were addicted to them. MPD police officers referred to the neighborhood as a difficult place for residents to "get out" of, to move to more affluent places. Perhaps coincidentally, it was also an analogy for the neighborhood's counterintuitive street grid plan with its many dead-ends and one-way streets.

Publicly available crime maps of Miami, drawing on police data and official statistics, consistently rank Overtown as one the most dangerous places in the city;[1] a reputation consolidated by media reports and academic research. In their chapter on crime and victimization, influential Miami scholars Alejandro Portes and Ariel C. Armony (2018) identify various typologies of urban crime, which they spatialize across the city. Differentiating between low-level street crime and more "ingenious" forms of delinquency such as fraud and money laundering, the authors warn their readers about the neighborhood: "Be careful: a wrong turn on the interstate can land you in the midst of Overtown, still a dangerous area" (2018: 84). While these typologies might be useful to capture a generalized and affective experience of crime, they do little to contribute to our understanding of how urban crime is spatialized in the first place. If anything, they tend to reproduce oversimplified and stigmatized representations of Miami neighborhoods and residents.

To move beyond such typologies, it is necessary to take seriously the racial and cultural politics through which crime is shaped, seen, and policed. This means attending to the ways policing, and the police in particular, create and reinforce urban inequalities and insecurities across Miami's geographies. In mainstream attempts to explain social relations and crime in a city, scholars and policy makers have used a racialized and quantified logic to map race and ethnicity onto the physical space. Many examine urban social problems through a spatial lens, focusing on the environmental and spatial conditions within a city or neighborhood. Crime in particular is often understood as directly linked to place of residence, suggesting that causes of delinquency should be found and addressed within the socio-spatial and cultural context of a local area and its population. Yet such theories are also thoroughly critiqued, as they largely ignore the ways in which political and economic factors have shaped metropolitan space and distributed residents alongside lines of race and class. Rather than being a "problem" of local residents and their environment, space is purposefully used to create inequality—a tool for racial exclusion and white oppression, and most notably, extreme policing practices. Nevertheless, the created interdependencies of race and space continue to be influential today in both research and policy, and used to advance a spatialized notion of "blackness-as-risk" (Rios 2020).

Examining everyday policing and related socio-spatial inequalities in Miami, this chapter shows how racialized and selective policing practices and policies strongly affect the experience of living and working in Miami. Here, I draw parallels with other major urban areas throughout the United States. Scholars working on Miami are often interested in the city as an American "frontier," as the site of various local cultural interactions and transnational relationships that often extend to Latin America. Yet Miami's history—much like that of most US cities—is rooted in "strict racial divisions between whites and blacks" (Gosin 2019: 3). And even though Miami is often celebrated as an American city "emblematic of the country's growing diversity" (2019: 4), residents are very much subjected to historical and present politics of race as any other American place. In Miami, this is particularly visible in terms of socio-spatial segregation of white and Black Miamians.

To account for the diverse experiences of policing in Miami's uneven and racialized geographies, I concentrate my analysis on three aspects of everyday policing in three very different but geographically close and interconnected parts of Miami: Overtown, Wynwood, and South Beach. Overtown is a centrally located, low-income neighborhood close to Miami's downtown district. As described above, it is locally known as an impoverished, high-crime area, where predominantly Black residents live. In 2015, the city commissioner, Keon Hardemon, summarized the image of the stigmatized area in a public meeting with local residents: "Overtown today is just a place where you can buy crack." During the Jim Crow era of racial apartheid, the neighborhood was known as "Colored Town": a small part of Miami where Black workers and artists were required to live. Despite this history of violent segregation, current residents also remember the neighborhood as having a vibrant past, especially compared with what it has become today. In the 1960s, city officials decided to construct an overpass of the I-95 highway directly through Overtown, displacing thousands of local residents and disrupting local businesses.

In 2015, I stood in front of local Bishop James Adams as he spoke to protesters marching against the development of the Miami World Center, a public-private space consisting of Luxurious apartment complexes, shopping centers, and places for entertainment and nightlife (see figure 1.1 at the beginning of this chapter). According to the developers, the location of the center was ideal: in the city that is the "gateway to the Americas," close to South Beach and the city's central business district, and surrounded by the best art and culture Miami has to offer. It was, however, also close, if not technically located in, Overtown. The protesters carried two large banners with them, on which they had written their demands: "Hire Overtown" and "End Segregation." Local residents felt excluded and insisted that they should also benefit from such urban development projects. These demands nevertheless exemplify how the structural factors and the distribution of power behind urban segregation and inequality are rarely directly identified as the main catalysts for inequality. While specific urban development projects have increased and cemented Miami's racial segregation and inequality, the protesters were suggesting that hiring Overtown residents would be a step toward inclusion and ending race-based residential segregation. Rather than contesting the development of the Miami World Center itself, the protesters demanded that they be part of it; even if "inclusion" meant no more than a temporary position as a construction worker, becoming an employee in a shop earning minimum wage, or the provision of free Wi-Fi in the vicinity of the center (another demand made by the protesters). By emphasizing socioeconomic opportunities and urban renewal, real estate developers and city commissioners tried to sell the belief that an exclusive real estate project such as the Miami World Center can also end segregation and promote a more inclusive urban community.

Bordering Overtown is the neighborhood of Wynwood, an increasingly popular area in Miami. With its art galleries, cafés, and restaurants, but most importantly its street art and murals, Wynwood attracts both local and international visitors and ranks among Miami's top attractions on various travel websites. Although small, Wynwood has become a brand, a synonym for Miami's "magical" transformation of empty and dead space into something new and exciting. Within the past decade, real estate developers have helped gentrify the neighborhood, turning the warehouses into art galleries where wealthy art collectors store and display their possessions to the public (Garcia 2017). These collectors have been a key factor in the neighborhood's rapid growth, which eventually led business owners to open shops and restaurants in Wynwood.

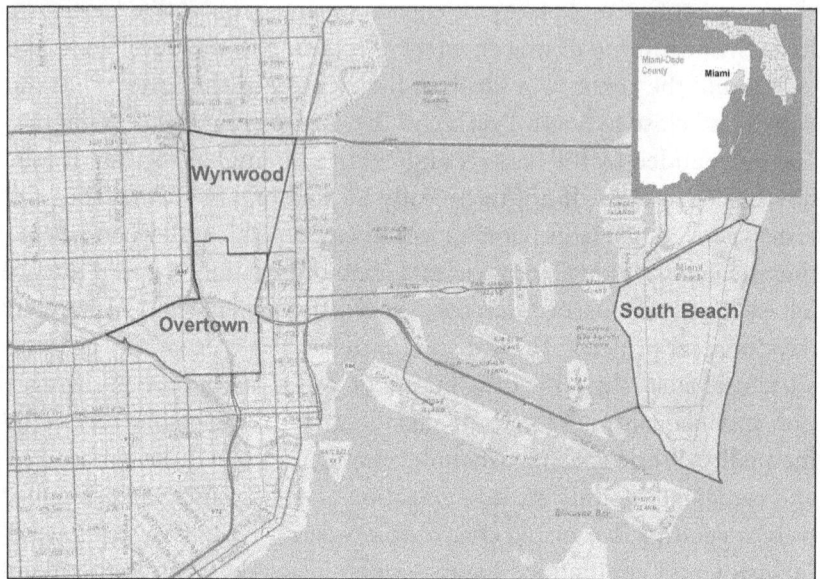

Figure 1.2. Map of Miami, including the locations of Wynwood, Overtown, and South Beach.

Today, Wynwood is known for being a young, energetic, and up-and-coming neighborhood, a place especially attractive for a younger public excited by its nightlife, dining, and shopping opportunities.

Many residents in Miami told me that South Beach is unlike the rest of Miami. Officially, the neighborhood is also located in Miami Beach, not Miami. In practice, however, the two are often perceived to be part of one metropolitan area, even though you have to cross one of three causeways to get from the mainland to South Beach and vice versa. South Beach is the most southern part of the Miami Beach island and is primarily known for its nightlife, art deco architecture, entertainment, and of course, the beach. Drawing on widespread spatial imaginaries of South Beach, residents told me that the neighborhood is representative of Miami's "superficial hype" and "over-the-top craziness." As we will see, it is also a neighborhood characterized by heavy policing. Police officers and private security guards constantly patrol the area, and their number drastically increases during certain events, such as Art Basel and Memorial Day weekend, and more recently, the policing issues and use of excessive force during spring break 2021. Such moments illustrate that South Beach is not necessarily an exception to the power relations and practices of policing seen elsewhere; it is indeed more similar to Overtown and Wynwood than many residents would like to believe.

The Police in Overtown

The City of Miami and the City of Miami Beach allocate around one-third of their budgets to the police: in 2019, this amounted to $265 million and $115 million, respectively. With these budgets, the cities have a respective total of 1,371 and 371 full-time sworn positions. Miami is divided into three policing districts, consisting of a total of thirteen neighborhoods. During my research, Miami Beach was also divided into three districts, though a fourth (with an exclusive focus on the entertainment area) has recently been added. Using a similar hierarchy as the military, the chief of police constitutes the highest rank in a police department, followed by major and commander, down to sergeant and police officer.

Both departments have come under scrutiny for various reasons, including violent, racist, and sexist acts and comments. Between 2008 and 2011, MPD officers intentionally shot at thirty-three individuals. After these shootings, the US Department of Justice (DOJ) conducted its second investigation into the department's practices and concluded that MPD officers had engaged in the use of excessive force, and that internal investigations remained inadequate. In a letter sent to the mayor and the chief of police in 2013, the DOJ wrote that it was deeply concerned that "many of the deficiencies that we previously uncovered now appear to be deeply rooted."[2] The agency recommended that the MPD improve accountability, in particular by modifying its policies and training. Skeptical of such promises of reform, and in light of growing calls to "defund the police," local journalists have pointed out that the City of Miami spends less than $6 million, or about 0.7% of its budget, on its Department of Human Services, which includes homeless outreach (Flechas et al. 2020). This is exactly the point of Alex S. Vitale, who explains that the police have become involved in a series of social problems that they cannot solve: "Police argue that residents in high-crime communities often demand police action. What is left out is that these communities also ask for better schools, parks, libraries, and jobs, but these services are rarely provided" (2017: 2). Despite these community needs, the police continues to be a well-funded public service available to the residents in these neighborhoods (even if not uniquely so), which signifies a clear disconnect in the provision of public services. It is important to stress how much money police departments receive compared with other public services, and that in addition, police officers are also expected to respond to a multitude of societal issues.

Once my drug and alcohol test came back negative, I was allowed to join a "homeless outreach" organized by the Housing Assistance Center (HAC) in Miami Beach as an official intern. In a large van, two HAC employees, two Miami Beach police officers, and I drove (and walked) around looking for people sleeping outside in the middle of the night. According to Melissa, the HAC supervisor present that night, there were 193 homeless people in their community, and some of them had recently became more aggressive. Before the actual outreach, we parked in front of the MBPD police station on Washington Avenue and waited for two officers to join us. "Sometimes," Melissa commented as we stood outside in the dark and empty streets, "officers don't come out, which happened a couple weeks ago." It did seem like a thankless task at the time, walking around from 3 a.m. to 8 a.m. to look for people sleeping in parks, alleyways, and playgrounds. "These people have offended the law, primarily because of trespassing or because of intoxication," Melissa explained as the officers tried to wake up a person sleeping next to a statue. "Nevertheless we are going to offer them help and assistance through Medication-Assisted Treatment [MAT] programs. If they decide they don't want to, then it's up to the police to decide what they want do with them." During the outreach, the police officers appeared visibly annoyed with their task, and their sudden shifts in demeanor (from aggressive to calm) suggested to me they were uncertain about which approach worked best with people who appear unresponsive or intoxicated but are otherwise no threat.

Just before we headed back to the HAC office, we entered Lummus Park: a place where many homeless people usually sleep and where residents who live nearby often complain about that to the police. We found five people sleeping on the beach, directly outside the park, on the other side of a stone wall. Officially, they were not trespassing the park. Nevertheless, they were sleeping on the beach and police officers debated whether the beach is "open," since the sun is not completely up (the beach is closed from dusk to dawn, as otherwise the police would have to patrol the beach at night as well). The officers woke the people up in the end and inquired whether they want to be admitted to the MAT program. Most of them declined and had to leave the area as soon as they packed their belongings. One resident from across the street opened his window on the second floor and gave a thumbs-up. The police officers were relieved; they will not receive any complaints from him today.

In general, police officers seemed concerned with public complaints and felt a strong need to "document everything to cover our tracks," primarily to protect themselves from litigation as well as to appear professional in front of a judge. This was important to them as, in their view, it could affect the extent to which legal professionals took their arrests and cases seriously. Yet these concerns often involved their working in wealthier neighborhoods with white affluent residents. In contrast, one MPD sergeant I interviewed echoed a broader sentiment that transparent, polite, and accountable policing does not work on residents in neighborhoods like Overtown. "I went on vacation," an MPD sergeant began his story. "It was on a cruise. My wife asked me if I wanted to go on a two-night cruise and we're out there in the middle of the ocean, we're sitting down for dinner, and of course, on a cruise ship, they seat you with other people, so you can make acquaintances. The woman across me, we're discussing what we're doing for a living, she asked me: 'What do you think about all the police brutality?'" As the police sergeant explained, he took a deep breath and sighed loudly. Annoyed by the question, he replied that the public wants the police to do a job without knowing how they do it. While he conceded that some officers have "behaved inappropriately," he suggested that the police badge, as a symbol of authority and power, is simply not enough for effective policing. "Many people," he concluded, "don't understand anything else but force." His frustration was not so much about the complaints he received, as about his discretion of when, where, and how to use violence in everyday policing.

While police diversity is unlikely to solve longstanding issues of anti-Blackness within policing and the criminalization of Black neighborhoods, it is noteworthy that the majority of police officers in the United States who patrol minority neighborhoods are white. In terms of police demographics, MPD officers are 82% male, 54% Latinx, 27% African American, and 19% non-Hispanic white (Leatherby and Oppel, Jr. 2020). Compared with the national average, police forces in Miami have a higher percentage of Black officers, yet in many Black neighborhoods the majority of the police are white. In Miami, the first Black police officers were hired in 1944, and the Black police precinct was built in Overtown in 1950 to house the operations of the growing Black police force. These officers were officially referred to as "patrolmen" and were not permitted to arrest white citizens without the presence of white police officers. The precinct closed in 1963, when it was integrated into the main MPD police station. The building currently serves as a museum, preserving and displaying the struggles and accomplishments of Black police officers in Overtown. One former officer currently works there as a guide. During a personal tour, he explained that back in his day, Black police officers had to be self-reliant and could not count on the city: "You had to fight for everything." Dealing with a widespread fear of Black crime, the former police officer did not blame people for pointing guns at him after they had just been robbed: "I was also a Black man entering your house." He remained very concerned with the policing practices seen today, and through his work at the museum, he hoped that "white officers learn to understand Black culture."

The former precinct building is also used for various community meetings, which often center on experiences with crime and the police in Overtown. During a meeting in March 2015, various politicians, residents, police officers, and activists from all over Miami, including Trayvon Martin's uncle, had come together to discuss the racial disparities seen in policing today. Referencing recent cases of police brutality in various US cities, they clearly understood Miami to be no different, and some indeed had their own experiences of police brutality to share. Speakers informed the audience of the disproportionate incarceration rates of African Americans compared with other racial groups (see also Garland, 2001; Goffman, 2014). One audience member rhetorically asked if anyone had seen a Black police officer shooting a white kid lately. Yet other members of the audience remarked that violence, both police brutality and "Black-on-Black crime," was often the outcome of individual behavior and a "problem of culture." A woman next to me explained that her sons never dressed in a certain stereotypical way: "My boys never drop their pants!" Another man followed up: "My grandson is going to Harvard!" These attendees implied that it was up to individuals to make sure their children did not become victims of violence in all its forms. "When Blacks become indoctrinated by internalized racism," Natasha C. Pratt-Harris and colleagues write, "they begin to see other Blacks as perpetrators of society's evils, rather than victims of white supremacy" (2016: 381). Any attempt to explain Black crime, in other words, must take into account the unique history of slavery and oppression, and must take seriously the workings of racial discrimination within the administration of justice.

A couple of blocks from the precinct in Overtown, Marcus and Fenix, both African American men, worked as hairdressers in a barbershop. Marcus was in his thirties and the owner of the shop, while Fenix was a bit younger and had been working in the barbershop for a couple of months when we met. The two also lived in the same apartment complex, where Marcus lived with his wife and young son, and Fenix with his aunt. I met Fenix in a nearby restaurant, where I was interviewing another resident. Fenix was interested in my fieldwork and became involved in the conversation about police practices in the neighborhood. He invited me to the barbershop, where he introduced me to Marcus. Both were interested in my research in Miami, and the barbershop became a place for me to hang out regularly. It proved to be an excellent place for ethnographic research: not only could Marcus and Fenix continue their work during our conversations, but I was also able to speak to a diverse array of customers, most of them residents of the neighborhood.

In early 2015, Marcus had to appear in front of a judge; he was accused of spitting at an officer during an arrest. According to Marcus, the MPD had used a police dog to search his car while his son was still in it. Marcus had reacted aggressively, to which the officers had responded with force and arrested him. It was then, Marcus tells me, that one officer had spat in *his* face and the others had "turned the other cheek" and even accused Marcus of spitting. "Living in Overtown today," Fenix shouted from the back of the barbershop, "means getting slammed by the police." While they both laughed, they also recognized that such practices are actually part of a longer tradition in the neighborhood. Ever since the Jim Crow era of apartheid, Overtown—previously called

Colored Town or the "Central Negro District"—has been heavily policed. In the nearby community center, an older resident in his sixties, with an interest in documenting the neighborhood's history, showed me a copy of a 1963 *Miami Herald* article titled "A Big, Significant Blob of Crime." The article describes how the registration of crime in Overtown amounts to one big blob of numerous little dots on a map. The police, in turn, "crack down hard."

Many Miami police officers I spoke with considered Overtown to be a good place to connect with Black residents such as Marcus and Fenix. MPD instructors organized neighborhoods walks as part of the training for recruits. Dressed in black pants, dress shoes, shirt, and tie, the recruits walked in the blistering heat, the sweat starting to show. Underneath the I-95 overpass, the instructor addressed the group of thirty-six recruits and explained the purpose of such community walks: "Don't expect real police work if you don't integrate yourself!" As we walked through the streets of Overtown, police recruits told me that "you never know what might happen, when a firefight might take place, and who can help you. If you meet the right people, they can actually help you instead of stealing your radio when you are pinned down and away from your car. You never know *who* you'll need." According to the instructors, policing is about creating a sense of responsibility and reciprocity, and learning how to treat people equally, whether they wear a suit or are homeless. "Some people here made bad decisions or had bad things happen to them. You are not better than they are." The sergeant proceeded by asking who among the recruits had ever worked a "real job," by which he meant working long hours at minimum wage. Many recruits raised their hands. "Good, you will have a better understanding of the lives of some of the residents here." These recruits, the sergeant implied, would hopefully be able to understand and respond better to their needs. One of the recruits pulled out a granola bar and gave it to a nearby man who had a pile of belongings in a shopping cart and other things scattered around the sidewalk. While some residents, when they saw the large group, exclaimed "God bless you!" others forcefully shouted "Fuck the police!" One resident even threw a plastic baseball from their balcony at the recruits walking below. As we walked past the barbershop that Marcus and Fenix worked in, I waved awkwardly. I wanted to be visible, to acknowledge my transparency as a researcher, without really being seen.

A couple of days later, I returned to the barbershop, curious to hear what Marcus had thought when he had seen the recruits, and ready to explain my difficult positionality as a researcher. Luckily, Marcus had no problem with me walking along, but he was quick to point out that there was only one Black recruit in the whole group. While he did not mind the walk itself, and even welcomed social interactions with police officers, he found the decision to include only one Black recruit in a class of almost forty laughable—and indicative of the MPD's lack of interest in actually addressing racialized policing practices.

Indeed, any attempts to tackle racial disparities in policing did not seem to go beyond the need to identify and recognize "cultural differences." For example, during their six months of training, police recruits had to follow a course titled Policing a Diverse Community, which aimed to make them aware of the cultural differences of the residents they would encounter during their work. The plenary discussion, however, quickly came round to a debate on racism and slavery. The handful of Black recruits suggested that slavery still has an impact on the United States today, that the position of Black Americans has never been truly rectified. Others reacted with frustration. One officer emphasized that in Africa, Black people had held slaves as well, and thus their marginalization was not necessarily the fault of white people. This officer also spoke of how many Black people in Miami have become successful, especially in music and sports. The instructor, a police officer born and raised in Curaçao (still part of the Kingdom of the Netherlands), was interested in my opinion and put me on the spot. Caught by surprise, I attempted to explain that this "evidence" of "Black success" is often selective, as many draw on examples of Black rappers and basketball players for the Miami Heat to downplay the role of race in broader inequalities.

Moreover, though I felt too uncomfortable to say this aloud during the course, I felt that such efforts to create sensitivity toward cultural differences do not address the ways in which white supremacy shapes how recruits are trained, drilled, and prepared for their everyday working environment. Police recruits and instructors often interacted in a militarized style and through commands. The recruits saluted me in the morning, shaved their heads, and created a flag using military and war symbols that came to represent their class. While the idea of police diversity training sounds progressive on paper, such courses do not teach "about the unequal access to services, white flight, the redlining of districts, and overall disinvestment in Black and Brown communities that impact the communities they will serve" (Beliso-De Jesús 2020: 144). Indeed, they do not seem to change the way police officers actually surveil and interact with Black Miamians.

During a ride-along with officer Leo in Overtown, he drove slowly and pointed to several individuals who were sitting under trees, on concrete walls, or next to one another on plastic chairs. "They are selling drugs," he said. "We can only take them in holding for a day, and they miss a day of income, but that's about all we can do. We cannot really stop it. People have rights, and though I know what they are doing—because what else would you be doing?—I cannot do anything." He added, "No matter how low you go, a decent person is not going to rob other people." One can always sell oranges or water, he added, as we saw several people doing at traffic lights. When we arrived at an intersection where several young Black men were sitting next to one another, Leo saw a bottle of alcohol on the ground between them and pulled over in front of them. He rolled down his window and started talking to them, asking them to have some respect by not drinking. "But what are we to do in our neighborhood?" they asked Leo, to which he responded: "Stop killing each other." One of the men scoffed at his remark and Leo got upset. He got out of his car, "Now you're talking shit." After delivering a short and aggressive speech about their decision to sit on the sidewalk and drink instead of working, Leo got back into the car and drove off. "People don't like us," he said after a while. I did not know what to say.

Such interactions speak to the experiences of Marcus, who felt that police surveillance and harassment had only increased after he was arrested and falsely accused of spitting. Marcus told me that he often saw undercover police cars with a license plate ending with the letter "X"—the mark of a government car—parked in front of the barbershop. During various conversations, Fenix also told me about the many times he saw Marcus flee inside whenever a police car would pull up on the sidewalk in front of the barbershop. Protected by the shop's locked door, police officers would not follow him inside and would eventually leave. Yet Marcus was growing increasingly uncomfortable with their presence. After several months, Marcus told me that he could choose between five years of probation or two years in jail. He was inclined to take the probation. Yet as he said this, he leaned back in his chair, lifted his feet off the ground and said "I cannot touch the ground" as his white sneakers walked through the air, mimicking how careful he would have to be to avoid getting caught by the intrusive policing practices in his neighborhood. Marcus maintained that he had been wrongfully accused, and that it was in fact the police officer who had spat at him and not the other way around. Consequently, both he and Fenix referred to the police as being like a gang, and one that operates with a code of silence. "Nobody stands up if a mistake is made, and nobody goes to his or her superior if they see anyone else making a mistake." Marcus thus decided to start recording his encounters with the police—a story that continues in chapter 4.

Wynwood's Public-Private Partnership

Luz was an African American woman in her mid-thirties and a police officer with the MPD, working four days a week in Overtown and one day a week in Wynwood. I met her early on in my fieldwork, as the executive director of the local Business Improvement District (BID) gave me a tour of the upcoming neighborhood. Unlike other police officers, Luz seemed receptive to the idea of having me around during her work in Wynwood. I quickly developed a friendly relationship with her, and I was able to discuss a range of relevant subjects with her, including sensitive topics such as police brutality and racial profiling. I met up with Luz regularly during my fieldwork. Together, we walked through Wynwood, enjoyed the air-conditioning in her car during hot afternoons, and spent time together at lunch cafés and bars outside of her working hours. Her experiences and insights were central to my understanding of the experiences and actions of police officers in Miami. As a Black police officer, Luz sometimes felt part of a general community of policing actors. But she also experienced increasing feelings of alienation and frustration, asking herself whether she was actually accepted as a full member of this professional community. To what extent can you feel part of the larger community of police officers if you disagree with some of your colleagues' main perceptions and actions?

During her work, Luz found it difficult to associate herself with people who were dedicated supporters of police practices, especially in light of the recent scrutiny of police brutality, both in Miami and the country at large. These critical reflections on her own position and work gave rise to feelings of alienation, which were strengthened through broader arrangements between various public and private policing actors and clients. In addition to her work as a patrol officer in Overtown, Luz also worked "off duty" in Wynwood. Off-duty police officers are not on active patrol for the police department but are assigned specific tasks while still enjoying the same rights and privileges accorded police officers. Various collectives, companies, and organizations pay these off-duty police officers' salaries indirectly, through the police department. At the time of my research, the MPD was usually paid thirty-five dollars an hour when regular officers performed off-duty tasks, while the presence of higher-ranking officers (per official policy when several off-duty officers were needed) and special circumstances (during holidays) involved an increased hourly rate. Even though off-duty police officers are paid privately and are not working on duty for the police department, an off-duty police officer still wears an official uniform, carries a police-issued handgun, and drives an official police vehicle. In Wynwood, police officers drive around the neighborhood with a Wynwood BID sticker attached to one of the side doors. The sticker notifies the public that these police officers are working for the BID, and that they are specifically (if not exclusively) concerned with any issues within the borders of Wynwood. Moreover, it suggests that the BID is able to inform these officers of their priorities during their shift, such as what to look out for and where.

Hiring off-duty police officers is a common practice throughout Miami and the United States in general. While off-duty officers are more expensive, many clients prefer them over private security guards. This is because police officers enjoy more rights: they can use force more liberally and can actually arrest people. Tim, the managing director for the Wynwood BID, told me during a tour of the neighborhood that they had decided to work with off-duty police officers to "cut out the middleman." In his experience, private security guards could do little more than call the police, whereas police officers could respond immediately. Police work is, furthermore, considered to be more prestigious compared with the work of security guards. In general, wealthier companies and organizations are more likely to make use of off-duty police officers because they can afford their salaries and because of their higher sociopolitical status—a status that is, in their view, more in line with the clientele they wish to attract. An indication of this differentiation is the fact that more expensive supermarkets such as Whole Foods and Publix use off-duty officers, while relatively cheaper stores such as Presidente hire private security guards.

In Miami, the use of off-duty police officers is particularly visible in Wynwood, a popular and upcoming neighborhood for art, shopping, dining, and nightlife. The dramatic growth of the neighborhood's popularity, which began in the early 2000s, was the direct outcome of a decision on the part of wealthy art collectors to store their collections in the relatively cheap warehouses in the neighborhood and open local galleries (Garcia 2017). In combination with the BID's successful branding strategies, art collectors caused the value of real estate in Wynwood to increase, attracting developers, business owners, and investors as a result. The directors of the Wynwood BID looked to expand and profit from the neighborhood's popularity, and after approval from the City of Miami, it was made compulsory for all businesses in Wynwood to make a collective contribution to the BID. BIDs, as one scholar explains, "are public-private partnerships, in which property and business owners in a defined geographic area elect to make a collective contribution to the maintenance, development and marketing/promotion of their commercial district" (Ward 2007: 658). Although the exact institutional arrangements and practices of BIDs may vary from place to place, such public-private partnerships have become an increasingly popular model in cities in the United States and elsewhere (e.g., Canada, Australia, and South Africa).

Primarily concerned with urban livability, BIDs implement policies which aim to "revalorize city centers and downtowns, to improve the 'business climate'" (2007: 668). The Wynwood BID oversaw the neighborhood's transformation from a relatively empty space with warehouses and poorly maintained real estate to one of Miami's most well-known areas in the space of a decade. Real estate developers and BID managers told me they envisioned Wynwood as combining elements of New York's Lower East Side district with a Dutch *woonwijk*, a place or pedestrian zone where people live and walk around. Cars drive slowly, and there are many crossovers. In doing so, developers and investors also forced existing tenants and unwanted businesses to leave in order to make room for newer restaurants, galleries, amenities, and shops.³ The documentary film *Right to Wynwood* tells the stories of tenants who were evicted or who could not afford the exponential increases in rent (Álvarez 2013). The documentary sparked a controversy, and its narrative was contested by investors and developers who claimed in conversations with me that Wynwood had always consisted of empty warehouses and no one had been pushed out.

From the start of its dramatic growth, local residents and developers understood Wynwood as being situated in a larger area with a reputation for being unsafe. Located directly north of Overtown, both actual incidents and any perception of crime would be likely to halt Wynwood's growing popularity. The BID was therefore preoccupied with providing what it saw as the necessary security services. While this did not involve the building of physical walls, the security arrangements and parallel public services set up in Wynwood showed similarities to Mike Davis's (1990) idea of the "fortress city" and Teresa Caldeira's (2000) concept of the "city of walls." These conceptions are concerned with the linkages between policing, private stakeholders, and the construction of the urban environment that divide cities into physical and social spaces populated by fearful middle and upper classes, on the one hand, and an increasingly marginalized underclass, on the other. In this case, the BID collected extra taxes from business owners in the neighborhood to pay for collective services, such as a cleaning crew, off-duty police officers, and private security guards. One of the most influential real estate developers in Wynwood and a BID board member told me that the organization had spent almost a third of its total budget of $700,000 on security in 2014. He wanted to increase this amount significantly in the coming years and aimed to invest in new surveillance cameras that could be operated and accessed remotely.

Luz generally enjoyed working in this charming neighborhood. She considered it a welcome change to her regular patrol, and it generated extra income. In Wynwood, she could drive or walk around without having to respond to the police radio and the dispatcher's calls. During these off-duty days, it was mostly up to her to decide where she wanted to go. However, she did carry a dedicated phone with her, and the BID provided the number of this cell phone to all business owners in Wynwood should they want to contact a police officer in a non-emergency situation. A "Wynwood cop," as off-duty police officers in the neighborhood were called, did not receive many calls on this number. Luz only occasionally had to respond to calls concerning a nuisance caused by an intoxicated or homeless person.

Through her work as an off-duty police officer in Wynwood, Luz became part of a public-private security partnership that shared the ambition of preventing and reducing crime in the neighborhood. "Tim is entitled to make demands because he pays," Luz explained to me. "So I'm basically a private security guard . . . Wait, no, that's not what I meant." She quickly corrected herself, recognizing that police officers still enjoy a higher sociopolitical status and additional rights. However, the formal arrangements of off-duty police work blur the boundaries. Both the MPD and the BID suggested that reducing crime required both the police department and the public-private partnership to actively collaborate and share information about past crimes and current and future threats. In monthly meetings, MPD commanding officers presented crime statistics and raised awareness among members of the audience (primarily consisting of developers, investors, and business owners) in terms of what made the neighborhood susceptible to crime. Police commanders explicitly stated that they required input from the Wynwood community to establish effective responses to various forms of crime that occurred in the neighborhood, such as armed robbery, burglary, vandalism, and murder.

A main outcome of these collaborations between the BID and the MPD was a specific description of people, situations, and locations, which was made available to local business owners and police officers. In practice, Tim and an MPD sergeant informed Luz of where in the neighborhood she should patrol, and what kind of individuals were of concern to them. After somebody had attempted to steal a designer handbag from a female pedestrian, for instance, Tim had asked Luz to be present in that particular area. In one meeting just before the schools closed for the summer, Tim told the audience that "kids are going to come out, around the age of twelve, thirteen, or fourteen, riding around on bikes in groups between five to forty, and all dressed the same, like a gang." In his perception, these kids could steal a phone or a purse, and when they left it would be impossible to identify who was the actual perpetrator. "We need to stay proactive," he informed the Wynwood collective. "Trust your instincts. If something doesn't feel right, or feels a little funny, call the BID number."

Luz understood that security was a key concern of the BID, and that the MPD looked to keep such lucrative clients satisfied. She also understood that working for the Wynwood BID was a desirable position. Compared with less interesting off-duty work, such as in a supermarket or at a construction site, being able to walk around freely in Wynwood clearly had its perks. Luz was therefore worried about whether Tim and her commanding officers were still happy with her performance. She sometimes called me after BID meetings, curious to hear if anyone had made any remarks about her or about anything else that could be of interest. Luz also tried to ingratiate herself with the area's many local and influential business owners, which was relatively easy for her. Many restaurant and gallery owners were happy to have a police officer around, and Luz in particular—many commented on her appearance as a young and attractive woman. In practice, this often meant receiving discounts and preferential treatment, such as skipping a line at a restaurant, which is also a common courtesy business owners give to police officers nationwide. One new restaurant owner offered Luz 50 percent off her order when she entered in uniform, and 20 percent off when she came in plain clothes.

On the one hand, Luz worked together with Tim and the BID to address "unwanted individuals" and "potential criminals," which were basically references to residents of Overtown and other nearby low-income areas. On the other hand, Luz also felt an affinity with African American and other Black residents, people who were considered by the larger society to be "not from Miami" and who were also targeted by police brutality. These conflicting loyalties created a complex situation for Luz, alienating her from some of the ideas propagated by BID members, while at the same time she had become increasingly attached to her off-duty job in the neighborhood. In Wynwood, business owners, restaurant managers, investors, police officers, and developers became part of a partnership that seemed to support racialized police practices almost unconditionally. Luz's everyday experience as both a police officer (a privileged profession) and Black Miamian (a marginalized race) was occasionally contradictory. While she was affiliated with the MPD, she also sometimes felt alienated because of the racialized security practices of her colleagues. Luz told me that she was not alone in her sentiment, and that many of her Black co-workers shared similar views but were too afraid to speak out in fear of retaliation.

Luz's story shows how public-private security arrangements develop and work at a local scale, with public actors such as the MPD pursuing private interests by enabling the hiring of off-duty police officers. Such arrangements have further institutionalized and reproduced segregation along the lines of race, both formally and informally, and more specifically by reproducing racialized practices and collectives beyond the institutional realm of the police. Sitting in her police car parked outside a restaurant, which had hired her services until 3 a.m., Luz could barely keep her eyes open. To keep herself awake, she started a YouTube video of a comedian on her phone—the police laptop does not allow external connections. Just before falling asleep in the parking lot, she wondered if she still wanted to continue working such hours.

Private Security in Miami Beach

In July 2014, an off-duty police officer hired by Mango's, a popular Miami Beach bar, was caught working under the influence of alcohol. Security cameras captured the officer with his handgun in his hand, showing it off to the bar's customers. After eight months of internal investigation, the department concluded that the off-duty officer had drunk at least six glasses of double vodka and cranberry juice, and he was fired in 2015 (though the MBPD was forced to rehire him in 2016 after his lawyer successfully claimed wrongful termination). In 2015, the *Miami Herald* printed the story and images from the video, scrutinizing the officer's actions and MBPD practices more generally, and questioning whether police officers should be able to work in bars. Daniel Oates, the MBPD's chief of police, took swift action and changed the department's official policy: police officers would no longer be allowed to work off duty inside South Beach bars.

Mango's, and all the other South Beach bars, found themselves in need of alternative policing actors. Rather than using their own security guards, these businesses preferred to hire guards from external companies. In addition to relying on private security companies' expertise, local businesses who used such companies could avoid having to deal with legal accountability should incidents take place: altercations between guards and customers would be the responsibility of the security company and not the business itself. Many bars decided to hire private security guards from Xecurity, a company owned and managed by Rick, an MBPD officer who was well known in the area. Rick told me that it had made sense for him to start a business "[in] the world that I live in. My experience as a law enforcement officer gives me the opportunity to train my employees in a particular and proactive way: my guys are going to deal with a situation before it becomes a situation, you know what I mean?" Rick suggested that with his skills as a police officer, he was well equipped to educate private security guards. In particular, he saw his individual perception of how threatening situations developed as useful for training his employees to be proactive in their work.

At Happy Hour on Ocean Drive, the same boulevard where Mango's was located, the owner kept a special dining area reserved for MBPD officers in an attempt to have an informal presence of the police throughout the day. Uncertain whether off-duty officers were allowed to return, the bar's management decided to hire private security guards from Xecurity as their replacements. One of them was Santos, a Cuban American security guard who worked long shifts at the bar, sometimes up to twelve hours straight, mostly sitting at the entrance. Santos explained to me that his job was similar to that of a police officer but "took place in a bubble," meaning that he was confined to a smaller and demarcated area. I got to know Santos through a police officer who was an acquaintance of one of my academic supervisors and who used to work off-duty at Happy Hour. After talking with Happy Hour's security manager, I was allowed to hang out with the security guards on my own terms. Santos worked long hours, often until three or four o'clock in the morning. There was not much for him to do, and together with other security guards at the bar, we discussed our professional and personal lives, bodybuilding, ate fried crickets (cheap and full of protein: the ideal bodybuilder snack), and marveled at Santos's customized motorbike with its mini-batwings on the side mirrors. Most of the security guards were concerned with their physique, making sure they obtained the idealized look of someone who could physically provide safety. I would meet Santos every one or two weeks. During these times, I would sit with him at the entrance to the bar or follow him as we walked around inside.

Several other private security guards, including instructors at private security companies, also framed their work as similar to that of the police. However, it was often very different in practice—private security guards did not enjoy the same sociopolitical status, legal rights, or financial compensation. Indeed, the police officers with whom I became acquainted often made fun of private security guards, derisively calling them "mall cops." Santos really wanted to become a police officer, a role that, in his view, was more valued by the wider public. Every night, he helped the MBPD to set up lighting around the police towers on Ocean Drive and chatted with the officers. He also bought personal items, such as a badge and a tactical belt, through which he sought to define himself as a policing actor. If a customer showed aggression or unwanted behavior in the bar, it was Santos's top priority to get the customer outside the bar as soon as he could without provoking them and inciting more aggression or violence. Santos called this act of talking to someone in order to get them to leave the bar "verbal judo." Should the customer physically attack him and he be compelled to respond with force, neither he nor his company would be held liable for assault or battery as long as the altercation occurred outside the bar. This would be a different story if the struggle developed inside the bar, in which case the customer could potentially sue Santos and his company, creating all sorts of legal and possibly even financial complications for them. This context led Santos to assert that he would only use physical contact within the bar as a last resort.

Although off-duty police officers were prohibited from working inside bars in South Beach, there was one exception: Memorial Day weekend. Every year during the last weekend in May, Miami Beach becomes the stage for a range of festivities and celebrations. The city's climate and reputation have made it an attractive place to celebrate Memorial Day as well as many other festivities, such as spring break, Art Basel, and the Ultra Music Festival. Traditionally, Memorial Day is a national holiday to commemorate those who have died while serving in the US Armed Forces. It has become a major tourist event in Miami, and city officials typically expect around two hundred thousand visitors over the weekend.

Santos already disliked most South Beach visitors and made racist and stigmatizing comments on regular evenings. For him, Memorial

Day weekend, also known as "urban beach weekend," was the worst (long) weekend of the year. More than spring break and Ultra, Memorial Day attracts a primarily African American and Caribbean American crowd. Although these groups always seemed to represent a significant proportion of the visitors to the bar where Santos worked, local residents understood Memorial Day weekend to be primarily for Black visitors. For many, this was also a reason to oppose the weekend and to criminalize those who attended, or to warn white attendees of potential trouble. In 2015, when I told my roommate, Olaf, that I was going to walk around Miami Beach during Memorial Day weekend, and that my parents were also coming over to visit, he laughed aloud. Like many other residents, he told me that he was going to stay as far away from the event as possible. Some even choose to close their businesses and leave the city for a couple of days.

Local residents, politicians, and journalists have perpetuated the weekend's negative reputation by interpreting any violence that occurs during the weekend as a direct consequence of the visitors it attracts. In 2011, several MBPD officers surrounded a vehicle that had hit multiple cars and come to a halt in the middle of the street. When the driver seemed unresponsive to their commands, they fired numerous shots into the car, killing him but wounding one another in the process. Many bystanders recorded the incident with their cameras, and even though MBDP police officers were responsible for lethal violence, the videos became a vivid reminder for local residents of what occurs during Memorial Day weekend in South Beach.

Allowing for such racialized interpretations, the City of Miami Beach and the MBPD prepare well in advance for the weekend. A wide range of organizations pass on information to local residents: universities notify their students by mail of upcoming arrangements, and news websites update their readers on the latest security developments and potential concerns. In the run-up to the 2015 Memorial Day weekend, a major issue for the authorities was how to prevent people with an arrest warrant or stolen vehicle from entering Miami Beach during the weekend. Police officers therefore prioritized controlling and redirecting traffic during the festivities. As a result, arriving by car from Miami (and there was no alternative) became both nearly impossible and very expensive (many parking lots charged customers one hundred dollars for the day).

The MBPD closed multiple lanes, reducing the traffic to one lane so that they could check every single car passing through. This resulted in a line of cars that covered the entire causeway to Miami Beach and stretched the more than five kilometers all the way to Downtown Miami.

Various agencies and organizations in Miami distributed a map (figure 1.3) in preparation for the weekend. I received mine by mail from the University of Miami, while other residents received one from their employer or from the public agencies they were affiliated with. The map showed what security measures the local authorities had implemented. It illustrated how traffic was being redirected (black arrows), and the location of the license plate reader (black circle) and roadblocks (red crosses). It also showed the position of security guards (light blue triangle) and the number of police officers permanently stationed at night (blue circle). As the map illustrated, there were police officers and security guards on almost every corner, as well as watchtowers and light towers installed alongside the boulevard, including in front of Happy Hour where Santos was working.

The policing practices during the weekend bore similarities to those of a military operation: there was an MBPD "mobile command center" (a large camper van with a satellite communication system) stationed on a corner on Ocean Drive, and police officers used the NATO alphabet to refer to the weekend, calling it "Alpha Bravo." Normally, the police officers' regular workdays were divided into three shifts, A, B, and C, with each shift consisting of ten hours. During the Memorial Day weekend, however, the day was divided into two shifts, which meant that officers had to work twelve hours straight. Although nobody was allowed to take the day off, the MBPD still did not have enough police officers to fulfill the necessary roles and positions during the weekend, and therefore had to hire additional police officers from other nearby departments to patrol Miami Beach.

During this Memorial Day weekend, I walked around with the American Civil Liberties Union (ACLU), a national human-rights organization. Volunteers from the organization joined the festivities and looked to make contact with police officers. Should any violent incidents occur (especially involving police brutality), these volunteers were there to witness them and document any violations of human rights. Armed with a cell phone with a camera and the ACLU app, with which I could

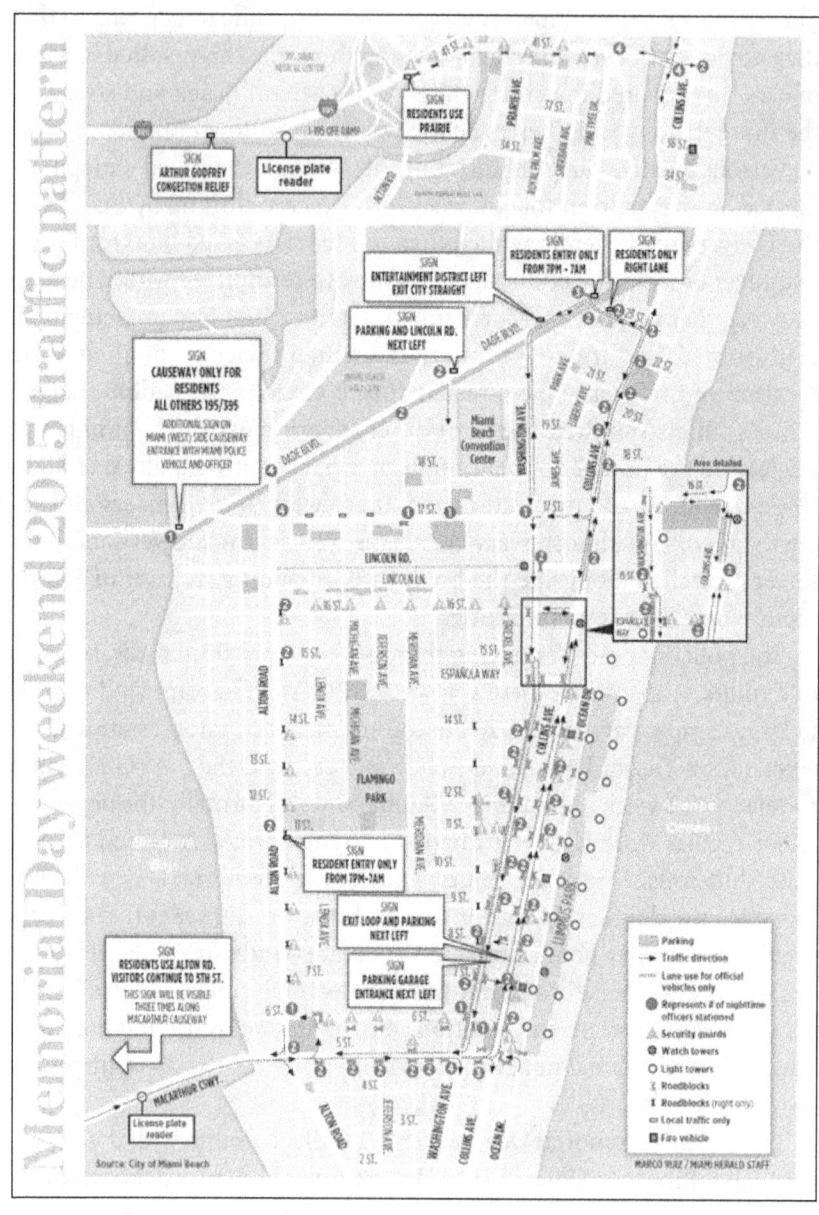

Figure 1.3. Memorial Day weekend 2015 traffic and security pattern, May 2015. Source: City of Miami Beach.

immediately upload any footage of a violent encounter to the organization, I joined several volunteers on Friday night.

As I walked past Happy Hour, I saw Santos sitting behind an officer who was checking the identification cards of customers waiting in line. This was usually his job, but since extraordinary security measures had been implemented for the Memorial Day weekend, he had been relegated to the role of backup security. It was busy and there was no way I could get through the crowd to talk to him, but I met up with him shortly afterward. Still exhausted, Santos told me how scared he had been, and that he understood why several other bars and restaurants had decided to close for the weekend. In his view, it was too great a risk, and indeed he mentioned the 2011 shooting in support of his negative opinion of the crowd that came to celebrate. In addition, he had also had a weapon on him to protect himself during the weekend.

Ever since the fatal shooting in 2011, the Miami Beach takes a "tougher stance" during Memorial Day weekend (Alvarez 2012). Journalists, residents, and activists have criticized the city for its racialized response, which includes more watchtowers, more officers, and more regulations. Despite such intrusive policing, however, the 2015 weekend was very peaceful and lively. Many visitors wanted to take a photo with the MBPD officers parked underneath the palm trees on Ocean Drive, most of whom willingly obliged. Luckily, there were no civil or human-rights violations for the ACLU to witness either. Sadly, in 2017, two men were killed, one of them shot by an MBPD police officer. In police narratives, a "successful" weekend means a lack of violence. Not only does this suggest that violence is expected, but also that police officers take credit for nonviolent weekends—implying that it is their presence, not the behavior and intentions of the Black visitors, that makes the weekend a success (Rivero 2013).

The heightened police presence during Memorial Day weekend illustrates how Miami Beach, with its reputation as a "paradise," can be easily transformed into a war zone occupied by foreign forces—but this is not a state of exception. The ongoing discussion of if and how Memorial Day weekend should be organized is not just about the hip-hop weekend in May. It is about how racial groups are policed differently, and how their presence, in the eyes of the authorities, requires additional policing to match the perceived security threat. For many Black Miamians, however, especially those who live in criminalized neighborhoods, these extraordinary measures are not exceptional at all but, rather, indicative of the continued attempts to keep Black people from driving over the causeway and using the city's beaches—a rule that was officially enforced until the 1960s.

Inequality and Insecurity

In 1967, the construction of the highway displaced over twelve thousand people and created a dark and empty space in the heart of Overtown, transforming the neighborhood's atmosphere. To compensate for this dead space and utilize it for something positive, city commissioners opted to create a playground for local children beneath the overpass. On the day of the playground's opening, Mayor Stephen Clark reassured the audience that Miami would not sweep its socioeconomic problems under the rug. While likely spoken with unintended irony, that day was richly symbolic for Overtown. During the opening, the grass—growing in weak soil and sparse sunlight—was already wilting, mirroring the expectations of Miami's poorer Black children who attended underfunded schools and had minimal access to city services. "[No one would] comment on the potential symbolism of a park that effectively rendered these kids invisible to travelers whisking above between the region's airports, beaches, and suburbs," Connolly (2014: 2) writes, as "the embodied future of black Miami looked up at a concrete sky." In 2018, conceptual artist Derrick Adams used original images from this playground in his piece during the Miami Art Week. His work, located outside a Miami Beach hotel, placed photographs of children playing underneath the I-95 overpass within a colorful installation and artistic impressions of playgrounds. Inserting this symbol of environment injustice and differentiated citizenship in a context of leisure, Adams told the audience he considered his work to represent a form of resistance: "To show play plucked from a history of oppression and disenfranchisement," Adams explained, "is a rebellious act" (Marvar 2018).

In late 2015, Dream Defenders organized a rally in front of the Stephen P. Clark Government Center—named after the mayor who had officially opened the children's playground underneath I-95. Dressed in T-shirts that read "Hire Overtown," I joined them as they entered the government building to make their demands known to city officials inside. Although some had entered an office and refused to leave despite repeated requests by police officers and security guards who followed us inside, it remained a peaceful event. Most officers who were called to provide backup did not feel that they had to intervene physically.

Foregrounding issues of urban safety and security, the stories discussed in this chapter speak to the experiences of many, both in Miami and elsewhere. By connecting local practices and interactions to broader trends in policing and socio-spatial inequality, I have shown how Miami is affected by a national context of exclusion and segregation. Both the public-private security arrangements in Wynwood and the securitization of Memorial Day weekend reflect broader US developments of privatization and racialized policing practices. In response, Dream Defenders rally support and organize protests in spaces that embody Miami's racial inequality and segregation. Activists have come to understand crime, policing, and violence in their city by connecting different geographical scales: protesters organized around the deaths of both Demz, a local graffiti artist, and Mike Brown, who was killed in Ferguson, Missouri, and who became a symbol of systemic state violence against African Americans throughout the US. Miami's racial inequality and selective security practices reflect endemic national systems of white supremacy and apartheid and are not an isolated issue or even an exclusively urban problem.

Unlike any other event, Memorial Day weekend shows how easily the idea of Miami Beach can be transformed from a glamorous tourist destination to a dangerous area, setting the stage for a form of policing that is, albeit perhaps only momentarily, suited to the "ghetto" (Jaffe 2012). In addition to socio-spatial inequality and the criminalization of particular neighborhoods, the event suggests that racial policing also has a strong temporal component: try crossing the bridge as an African American on the last weekend of May. Such aggressive and selective policing practices are indicative of a broader idea that transparent, polite, and accountable policing does not work on certain population groups. Such policing tactics, as Erika Robb Larkins (2018) also explains, are grounded in the idea that some portions of the population deserve unchecked violence. Thinking "beyond traditional public/private divides" (2018: 149) in policing, Larkins shows how such events "further bifurcated security practices in an already divided city" (2018: 139). Similarly, the Memorial Day weekend in Miami, though on a different scale, exemplifies and intensifies the racialized experience of policing in the city—past and present.

Yet my analysis of everyday policing in this chapter involves more than alluding to the exclusive logic of policing and the production of socio-spatial differences. Examining the interdependencies between race, space, and everyday policing, we can begin to identify how vigilant citizenship emerges in Miami—a segregated urban space with a pluralized and privatized security landscape. This is a landscape characterized by not only numerous public and private actors involved in the provision of security but also widespread feelings of *insecurity*. For many living and working in the Miami neighborhoods discussed in this chapter, dealing with (perceived) insecurities and negotiating their own safety has become part of their daily lives and professions. As a police officer herself, Luz felt uncomfortable affiliating herself with larger pro-police collectives, and experienced difficulties in dealing with colleagues who used violence indiscriminately and unapologetically. Santos's explicit comments about the dangers posed by the largely Black crowd on Memorial Day weekend speak directly to the relationship between the privatization of security and racist policing. He, too, experienced insecurity, and he reacted to these feelings by illegally carrying a gun on him during his working hours—a decision I will discuss in more detail in the next chapter. Finally, in feeling the threat of police violence and injustice, Marcus and Fenix also considered their own responsibilities: what could they do to escape state surveillance and the penal state? These nuanced understandings of inequality and insecurity, stories of low-paid security guards, exhausted police officers, and citizen responsibility, form the basis for the coming chapters, in which I focus on how vigilant citizenship shapes an engagement with surveillance, guns, and cameras in policing.

2

Do the Right Thing

When Paco realized that I was walking on a busy street, he told me to speak quietly. His voice on the other end of the phone, however, increased in volume as he expressed surprise at hearing me talk in public about the activities of his Citizens on Patrol (COP) group. I had met Paco during the MPD training program for Miami residents who wanted to learn how to patrol their neighborhoods—how to observe and report suspicious activities to local authorities. Since I was not a US citizen myself, I could not officially become a COP, but I could still participate in the classes. After talking about my research, Paco had allowed me to join his group as a student-observer. He was especially happy when I offered the use of my rental car for a day.

Figure 2.1. Miami Police Department police officers look for information after the murder of Marlon Eason in Overtown, March 2015.

A week later, I met Paco's COP group in front of a Presidente supermarket in Allapattah, a predominantly Latinx neighborhood adjacent to Overtown. Paco was there—with him I spoke both English and Spanish—and two others who spoke only Spanish. Once we had all taken a seat in my three-door red Toyota, the three of them began explaining to me what they observe and how they take notes. The MPD had provided them with a worksheet to fill out every week. Paco took a postcard from my parents out of the glove compartment and used it as a ruler to draw an extra line on top of the worksheet, on which I had to write my name since there was no room next to theirs. We made sure to put "participante/estudiante (participant/student)" next to it, so that there would be no confusion as to my status (we did not want to break official policy). The worksheet was new and the columns of "date," "time," "location," and "activity" were all still empty. Paco attached the worksheet to a clipboard, and we began our patrol.

En route to our first "stakeout," Paco and the two others showed me their badges. One of them was using a clean, black leather case to hold a shiny silver badge stating "Citizens on Patrol" and "Miami Police." Next to it was an identification card with his photo. I assumed that they all had their IDs with them in case local residents confronted them about what they were doing, yet they explained that it was to justify their "patrol" to police officers, who might wonder what they were up to.

"Los viernes son buenos (Fridays are good)," said Paco excitedly, adding in English that many people spend their money at the end of the week, and so this is when most things of interest to the COP group happen. Following his specific instructions, I parked the car in an alley overlooking the backdoor parking lot of a nearby supermarket, next to several dumpsters full of trash. Just a few minutes later, a heated argument began nearby among a group of ten to fifteen men. We lowered the windows of the car and gathered that the dispute was about money. One of the men claimed that he had been robbed by some of the others and wanted his money back. Some of the men began to push him away. Some were without shirts, and we could see a handgun sticking out of one man's belt. When the man claiming to have been robbed eventually left the scene, Paco immediately asked me to start the engine and drive backward through the small alley. We parked again a little farther down the main road.

Paco pulled out his cell phone and called a man he referred to as "Capi," short for Captain. Capi was in charge of the COP group, but since he was a little older than the others, he often remained at home, where he functioned as the link between the MPD and the COP patrol group. Paco informed Capi of what we had just seen in the parking lot; Capi in turn called the direct number for the MPD police commander of Allapattah. Later, Capi called back and told our group that the commander would be sending a nearby police officer to have a look or would at least inform the police dispatcher of the situation. Paco explained to me that we would have to get away from the area before Capi could notify the police; after all, we did not want anyone to know that we were collaborating with the police, that we were also surveilling and patrolling the streets, as this could jeopardize our own safety as well as the potential to covertly observe everyday crime.

During the rest of the COP patrol, we drove around a lot. Paco seemed to know his way around and was very specific in telling me where to go, how to drive, and where to stop. We observed several people whom the group believed to be involved in local drug dealing. A woman and a man repeatedly walked back and forth between a corner on the sidewalk and a back alley. Paco got out of the car to buy some candy from a nearby store and wrote down in great detail his observations of the "drug deals" before us. Again, we called Capi, but this time we also drove by his house and described the dealers in detail using another document provided by the MPD, which explained how to "describe a person": what clothes they had on, their hair color, their race, and so on. Capi lived in a one-story house with a large American flag in the front yard. He walked with a stick and leaned inside the car to introduce himself to me. Although we were not allowed to carry weapons during the patrol, Capi was happy to show me his gun, kept in a holster that showed through his white polo shirt. We eventually decided that we had observed enough for the day, and Paco urged me one more time to remember that our work was not to be discussed with anyone: "Mi familia, mi novia, o mi amigos—nadie! (My family, my girlfriend, or my friends—nobody!)"

The COP program is a voluntary service offered and promoted by police departments throughout the United States. During the COP training organized by the MPD, police officers encouraged residents to become the "eyes and ears" of the police. The MPD community-relations officer leading the training considered herself to be a good example of community-relations office: she knew everybody in her area, and other residents notified her when there was a strange car in front of her house when she was away. "Although it was my uncle with a moving truck, it's still an example of how you can help each other," she explained. "Pedophiles are found everywhere," the officer continued, producing an expression of light shock on the faces of the participants, "and they not only prey on young girls, but also on boys, and even the elderly. Yes, it's terrible, but you want to know what and who you are dealing with. You want to be 'ahead of the game.'" Police officers explained that the input and work of local residents would make their work much more effective, and that such resident participation is essential for preventing and responding to everyday forms of crime. "You can't give up on communication with the police—that's when the criminal wins," another MPD police officer explained during the COP training.

In addition, police officers explained that local residents should exercise their rights. "I'm sorry to say," the MPD community-relations officer told the group of participants, "but y'all pay our salary. It's not fair for you when you don't receive the right services." The officer continued by asking, "What do you need to become a police officer?" She promptly answered her own question: "A high school diploma." This was her way of suggesting that the requirements to become a police officer were not particularly high. She also said that the actions of police officers should not be explained by their education or training (or lack thereof) alone, but mostly by their personality, by who they are as individuals, and that "there are good and bad police officers." She continued, "And you as citizens have a lot of power: you should take the first step in reporting any problems to police officers." Before the end of the training, the officers shared a final piece of advice: "Watch the hands of people, not the eyes—the hands are what kill you."

This narrative—that the police depend on the input of local residents—was repeated throughout the various crime-watch meetings I attended in Miami, and it was one of the reasons why citizens were encouraged to learn how to become a citizen on patrol. Yet police officers also stressed that citizens should be careful. While COPs had to learn how and what to observe, they also needed to understand that under no circumstances could or should they confront criminals or enforce the law themselves. The officers gave some tips on how to secretly record others with a cell phone, but they also stated that COPs do not enjoy the same rights as police officers. COPs will be held liable in case they use violence or break the law in any way: "We have firms, laws, and unions fighting for us—you do not," the MPD officer summarized.

Programs such as COP are a form of "citizen mobilization": they use and rely on citizens to collaborate with police officers to deal with a range of security concerns, both domestic and international. Such collaborations are also known as "lateral surveillance": a form of surveillance in which citizens watch and report on one another to the authorities (Reeves 2012; 2017). The concept of lateral surveillance is useful for unpacking how citizens have been recruited for policing practices, and for understanding the concomitant shift in responsibility for security and how this is framed in terms of belonging to the nation-state. Citizens have been mobilized for surveillance purposes throughout US history, and the academic literature has long documented lateral surveillance programs and practices. Much attention has been given to neighborhood-watch groups, and their relationships with authorities in particular. My interest, however, lies in addressing how people experience and articulate these forms of lateral surveillance in terms of their rights and responsibilities as vigilant citizens in the context of everyday policing. How do relationships between state agencies, local communities, and individuals shift when the gathering and disseminating of knowledge about other citizens becomes framed as an essential duty of citizens?

There is, of course, nothing inherently wrong with somebody calling the police to deal with individuals or groups who jeopardize public and private safety. However, the solidarity rooted in actions of lateral surveillance speaks primarily to an idealized political community. These assumptions shape citizenship in terms of overlapping and conflicting allegiances to the nation-state, on the one hand, and to local communities, on the other. This idea of lateral surveillance involves attempts by police officers to convince residents, especially those living in low-income neighborhoods, that sharing information is an act of "good citizenship." As state agencies consider informants to be a crucial tool in fighting all kinds of criminal organizations and terrorist networks, they emphasize the contributions of a community of vigilant citizens to public safety. As explained before, vigilant citizens are watchful and are expected to report anything that has a whiff of illegality. Specifically, my analysis of such actions and experiences allows me to discuss what it means to *do the right thing*, and how vigilant citizenship is articulated through lateral surveillance. The cases of lateral surveillance that I discuss in this chapter reflect on how the police aims to convey to citizens that their involvement is essential for an efficient criminal justice system.

Proponents of lateral surveillance suggest that the authorities, given the opportunity to investigate, will make assessments of guilt and innocence in a legal and just fashion. Yet the practice is shown to have many downsides, and in fact it compromises the justice system and endangers the lives of those involved (Natapoff 2009). In practice, citizens might also be reluctant to collaborate, a practice colloquially referred to as "snitching." They might distrust local police departments, considering them incapable of providing security, or they may even experience their presence and involvement as the actual source of their insecurity. Moreover, lateral surveillance programs are likely to cultivate feelings of distrust, fear, and alienation among residents themselves, eroding community cohesion. This directly feeds into already racialized and violent reactions by police officers and neighborhood-watch members, as vigilant citizens interpret and investigate suspicious behavior through what scholars have called "normative whiteness": contextualizing situations and actions through racial categories that generate forms of privilege and disadvantage (Hurd 2008).

Lateral surveillance sustains and intensifies a range of historically racist discursive practices, which are grounded in a broader fear of Blackness that manifests in and beyond the institutional realm of the police. Black citizens in particular not only find themselves targeted by such practices, but they also experience difficulties when trying to connect with political communities across different scales. In the context of Florida, and in particular the stand-your-ground law, the murder of Trayvon Martin in 2012 by neighborhood-watch captain George Zimmerman stands out as a particularly horrific example of the ways many Americans think about crime and criminals. Zimmerman argued that he acted in self-defense, and his lawyers successfully presented Martin, who was in fact an unarmed Black teenager, as potentially threatening to a jury. As such, "Zimmerman's actions against Martin are far from surprising; they seem rather, to be a logical outgrowth of existing widespread prejudice and large-scale acceptance of racial profiling" (Johnson et al. 2015: 19). While the stand-your-ground law made it easier to justify Zimmerman's right to defend himself in a court of law, the broader administration of justice—and in particular the lack thereof for people of color—is indicative of a longer and racialized way of seeing and representing young Black men as suspicious and dangerous. It is the aim of this chapter to show how lateral surveillance shapes these acts and experiences of racial profiling, not only as extremely violent and lethal encounters but also as everyday articulations of vigilant citizenship.

Public Vigilance

During the First World War, several public vigilance campaigns emerged in the United States. State agencies created posters and distributed them among residents, who were instructed to watch out for and report "suspicious activities" especially by Black people. Government agencies aimed to create a kind of resilience and a general level of preparedness among their constituents. Residents were expected, encouraged, and required to be vigilant, to develop a heightened alertness and awareness of their surroundings. As a result, people were monitored by not only public and private organizations but also one another. In Orwell's dystopian classic *1984*, the main character Winston Smith is afraid of not only Big Brother and its technologies and employees but also his fellow citizens, who monitor one another and report "symptoms of unorthodoxy" (Larsen and Piché 2009: 187). In light of recent perceived terrorist threats, discussions of such "citizen mobilization" have only become more common. As a nation-state, the United States has a long history of mobilizing its citizens against a variety of perceived enemies, both domestic and international. Practices of vigilance, suspicion, and snooping have become rooted in US society and culture (Reeves 2017). People like George Zimmerman feel that it is their civic duty to scour their surroundings and respond whenever they identify something or someone as suspicious. Zimmerman's actions can therefore be understood through this lens as an act of citizenship. This duty of vigilance, the impulse of citizens to police one another, is more "socially destructive than the merely symptomatic threats of crime, petty immorality, and terrorism" (Reeves 2017: 180).

Recent analyses of surveillance have shifted to focus to digital technologies, which surpass human capacities in both speed and scope. However, while such technologies—e.g., the video camera—might dominate the security landscape, a purely technological view of surveillance limits our understanding of it in terms of citizenship and the formulation of political critique. People, in other words, are still the agents of surveillance. This explains why lateral surveillance programs are becoming increasingly popular: people are able to uncover and interpret intelligence in ways that most common (digital) surveillance technologies cannot, which is why citizens are mobilized to complement them (Reeves 2017). In other words, government agencies are convinced that citizens are good at observing one another and will report on one another to the authorities.

Lateral surveillance programs can easily be connected to the workings of the nation-state. Here, vigilance, and in particular vigilantism, is a result of neoliberal governance and the privatization of public services. Citizen patrols and vigilante lynching can be explained as a result of the government's failure to administer justice and provide security for its constituents (Goldstein 2015). Yet with or without the support of state agencies, civic participation in policing sustains a form of differentiated citizenship, in which some residents have access to these programs, while others do not. In turn, police officers and city officials tend to give more active groups more attention, generating "friendships and professional connections that streamlined and personalized police services" (Cattelino 2004: 123).

In Miami, I observed how residents were notified of their responsibility to collaborate with the police in various ways, especially through the news media. Local 10 News, a popular broadcaster in the metropolitan area of Miami, had a special item called "Get Them Off the Streets." In this item, a special crime reporter informed the audience of any local residents who had broken the law and were wanted by local police departments. He introduced the cases and urged viewers to contact authorities should they have any relevant information. I transcribed the item that was broadcast on May 28, 2015, as follows:

From a heroin dealer to some very dangerous drivers, they are all out there and we need to "get them off the streets" [as the large text behind the anchorman indicates]. Here's crime specialist John Turchin [camera switches to John]. Some are hardened criminals, some could still find the right path, but all of them are accused of breaking the law. So, let's help police get them off the streets. All right, we're going to begin tonight with this guy, Kristopher Barlitt. Take a good look at him. He's from Davie, he's accused of driving under the influence, but never showed up for court. Next on the list, Keith Clark, he's wanted for trying to pawn stolen property. Clark is from the North Palm Beach area, if you see him make that call. How about this guy, Roberto Guerrero. He's a Miami boy and an alleged pot dealer, but he's on the run right now. Let's try to find him. Our next fugitive is this guy, a babyfaced-looking guy that is, his name is Gordon Council. He's only twenty-one but wanted for grand theft. He was last seen in Islamorada. And you've got to help cops get this guy, Delarrian Black, Sr., he's accused of a whole lot of things including dealing both heroin and opium. He needs to be locked up, folks. Another guy from the Florida Keys, Scott Purvis, he's wanted for driving under the influence as well and used to live in Tavernier. Also, and finally our last one, a woman, Laura Ann Rager. Well, cops say she's trouble, folks, wanted for her third DUI and assault with a deadly weapon. It's time Rager sees the inside of a jail cell. OK, now remember now, the police need your help to get them all off the streets, and here are some of the numbers to help you remember: Miami-Dade Crime Stoppers, 305-471-TIPS, Broward County Crime Stoppers 954-493-TIPS, and you can see all these guys again, and this woman, on local10.com. I'm crime specialist John Turchin, Local 10 News (Local 10 News 2015a).

Like John Turchin, police officers, journalists, and local politicians consider the involvement of residents necessary to provide law enforcement with probable cause and legal evidence, and in so doing enable police investigations and legal prosecutions. This is not to say that, without citizen help, police officers would be completely unaware of criminal activities. It is, for instance, widely known by police officers, residents, and even movie directors that drugs are dealt and used in Overtown. Hollywood producers and directors also reproduce this common knowledge in popular culture, as in Sonny Crockett and Ricardo Tubbs' visit to Overtown to look for illegal drug transactions in the motion picture *Miami Vice* (Mann 2006). To pursue judicial action, however, state agencies need local residents to actively share information with them.

To encourage local residents to do so, the police have attempted to influence the legal dynamics that frame such political and contested forms of knowledge. The US government has changed federal law to protect those who participate in lateral surveillance. Before such measures, whenever a person falsely accused someone of terrorism, for example, the accuser would risk legal prosecution. This changed, as the act of "saying something" was increasingly framed as a duty of citizenship, and lateral surveillance was identified as a means to counter domestic acts of terrorism and organized crime. Especially after 2011, when the See Something, Say Something Act of 2011 was introduced and passed through the US Congress, US citizens became protected from libel action should they falsely accuse their peers (Reeves 2017). The idea behind this shift was straightforward: the law needs to protect those who have a vigilant mindset, instead of discouraging and punishing them.

A Slice of Citizenship

In a strongly air-conditioned conference room at the MPD, children and their families gathered with numerous police officers for the Do the Right Thing (DTRT) award ceremony. During this monthly ceremony, the MPD issues awards to children for their good citizenship and to police officers for extraordinary deeds performed in the line of duty. Campaign leaders nominate and award children and officers whose behavior they consider to be exemplary for their peers. Once everyone in the audience was inside, the ceremony began with the Pledge of Allegiance to the US flag on display on the podium at the front. A commanding officer then introduced the different cases and presented the individuals who had been nominated, including a police officer who, while responding to a different situation, had gone beyond the call of duty to save a man who was choking and a young girl who had proactively assisted a police officer when her friend had run away from home. In many cases, the nominees had shared secret information with local authorities without the consent of other residents. That month's award winner was the young girl mentioned above. Although her friend had told her about her plans in secret and had explicitly said that she should not tell anybody, the girl had nevertheless notified her friend's parents and police officers. The involved police officers explained that they had been able to respond promptly and bring the runaway girl home before anything could happen to her. The audience applauded as family and friends took pictures of the girl with the involved police officers at her side, with the US flag in the background.

The DTRT campaign was an official part of the activities of Miami's police departments, and it was financed through confiscated drug money. It usually received around $1 million per year and was specifically set up to involve children in primary and secondary schools, much like police school visits and other community-relations programs to acquaint children with law enforcement, including "Officer Friendly." In an interview, the founder of DTRT told me its aim was to improve "relationships between the youth and the officers" in the city. During the summer, campaign leaders believed it was especially important to keep children from hanging around and thus getting into trouble. Police officers would therefore hand out coupons for free pizza to young people whom they felt had displayed behavior that was reflective of good citizenship. MPD police officers explained to me that "being a good citizen" in this case generally involved an active collaboration with law enforcement officers. The coupon, as shown in figure 2.2, was jokingly called a "citation," but instead of having to pay a fine, the recipient could get a free pizza from Papa John's Pizza Company.

The DTRT campaign illustrates how the relationship between police officers and local residents is framed in terms of good, and thus vigilant, citizenship. It suggests that the duties of the ideal type of citizen include informing and collaborating with the authorities. MPD police officers and DTRT campaign leaders suggest that such actions should be rewarded. Likewise, the various neighborhood-watch groups and captains I contacted in my research often aligned themselves with police officers and called on the police—framing them as an underfunded public service—to ramp up their policing practices in their neighborhoods.

The first crime-watch group meeting I joined took place in Coconut Grove, a wealthy neighborhood next to Biscayne Bay. I wore shorts and a white T-shirt and arrived a bit sweaty from the bike ride. I got the impression that my appearance was not exactly what the participants,

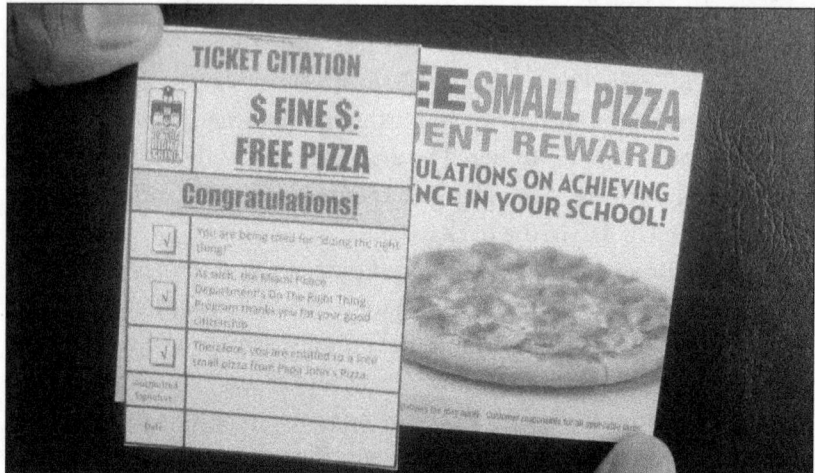

Figure 2.2. A "ticket citation" from the Miami Police Department providing free pizza, August 2015.

still dressed in office attire, had in mind when they heard that a foreign researcher was coming that evening. But once I had settled in between the thirty or so residents and stakeholders in the local air-conditioned church, Susan warmly introduced me to the group and said that I was welcome to attend their monthly meetings. As the group's chair and a long-term Coconut Grove resident herself, Susan explained that she was "fighting for every single resource we deserve, what our rights are."

Over the course of several months, I saw how members of the crime-watch group and MPD police officers shared phone numbers, discussed information about crimes and criminals, showed pictures of suspects and videos of suspicious activities (Susan said she once recorded a drug deal in front of her home while hiding in her car), and explored possible judicial procedures to address feelings of insecurity and nuisances such as overdue maintenance and poor lighting. Neglecting larger structural conditions of inequality, participants in the meeting concluded that "even though someone is poor and addicted, he doesn't have the right to break in." While many encouraged Susan to announce her successes more widely in order to attract additional funding and generate political support (there were already fourteen hundred people on her mailing list), she was reluctant to seek publicity. In part, she feared the repercussions, but she was also afraid that she would give other residents the impression that the group was taking the law into its own hands. Especially in light of what had happened to Trayvon Martin, she worried that they, too, would be considered vigilantes. Of course, Susan assured me, this was not what she envisioned her group to be.

Most participants at these meetings were white or Latinx and shared stories that reproduced dominant and racist interpretations of crime and belonging that criminalized predominantly Black communities and citizens. During one meeting, participants discussed a recent event that they referred to as a "roadside rampage": young Black men had driven from a more "crime-ridden" neighborhood to Coconut Grove, committing a series of crimes along the way, before finally crashing their car in their community. In the story, as told by these participants, the men had also stolen body armor and a handgun from an unlocked police car. These unintended revelations of racism, and in particular the narratives of who belongs in a neighborhood, are anchored in ideologies of maintaining cultural "whiteness" (Low 2004: 150). This is particularly salient in terms of the rapid increase of Americans living in secured residential enclaves and gated communities, the creation of which is often shown to sustain and intensify discriminatory policing practices and existing patterns of segregation as ways to defend white privilege. Yet beyond the walls of these gated communities, as the example of community policing in Coconut Grove illustrates, a broader search for safety and security reorganizes American communities around a fear of specifically Black crime.

During these neighborhood-watch meetings, it struck me how most of those participating also emphasized the importance of individual responsibility and the rule of law. Victims of crime themselves were often considered to be "irresponsible," as they should have known to avoid being in a certain area at a certain time, or should have locked the doors of their car. Safety, in other words, was often framed as the outcome of rational and responsible decision-making. Furthermore, the group members believed that without their personal involvement, policing would be less effective, the criminal justice system would be less efficient, and their communities would be even less safe. At the same time, many nevertheless felt insecure in light of general perceptions of crime, as well as due to fear of the potential repercussions of their collaborations with the police. Several participants expressed a fear of gang activity in the neighborhood, and one woman said that she had hidden in her bedroom with a pistol for hours during a power outage, afraid of potential intruders.

Many high-ranking police officers—including the MPD Chief of Police, Rodolfo Llanes—attended these crime-watch meetings and praised the group members for their efforts. The group's successes, such as lower crime rates, higher arrest rates, and additional funding, were celebrated and held as exemplary for other crime-watch groups throughout Miami. City officials and lawyers looking for votes were eager to present their work during the monthly crime-watch meetings, and high-ranking police officers seemed pleased with the group's activities and involvement. Another neighborhood-watch captain in Miami Beach, Mia, a Latinx resident in her forties, explained to me that "most police officers I've met are decent people, and the stigma has prevented people to join the police." One of the things she had requested was a neighborhood policeman

> who, you know, just drives around at night. But what it does is create a feeling of safety for people—even if the cop is a corrupt cop, it's still a cop! And if somebody came over to me dressed like you, as you are right now, for the benefit of the interview in a T-shirt and shorts[1], and you said to me, put your hands up—any man in a uniform would deter such crimes.

In light of a growing critique of police presence, Mia emphasized that officers are crucial for public safety. And as the neighborhood-watch captain in her neighborhood, she felt responsible for developing and maintaining a good relationship with the police department and officers working in the area.

One day I found a flier in the mail announcing the first meeting of a new local crime-watch group founded by one of my neighbors, Alejandra. As the group's captain, Alejandra went on to organize several monthly meetings, during which police officers and local residents exchanged information, expressed concerns, and discussed possible solutions to security issues. After attending several of these meetings, I talked to her about how and why she had set up the group, and especially how it had affected her relationship with other residents and police officers living and working in the neighborhood. Alejandra told me that the authorities had been unresponsive to her reports of the threats and her concerns about general safety in the neighborhood. I asked her how the police had initially responded to her initiative to start a crime-watch group in the neighborhood. She explained:

> I had a little fender bender in Miami Beach and the cops arrived in two minutes. I could not even get anyone here during a shooting. I could not even get anyone here during a shooting! I work in the judicial system, I asked them: "Where are the [forensic] technicians to take evidence? My neighbors' tires have been blown out, all the shell cases on the ground. Where are the technicians? Where are the officers? Where is the investigation?" You know what he told me, the cop? "Do you have a gun?" That's what he asked me: "Do you have a gun?" And I am looking at him, saying, "What do I need a gun for? You are here." He goes, "Well, you should have a gun. You should move to the other side [of the city]." And the lady officer that was with him said, "Yeah, I moved to Pembroke Pines. You should do the same. You want to get out of here."

In addition, Alejandra told me that she had received multiple threats from other residents after she decided to set up the crime-watch group. According to her, some criminal neighbors felt threatened by her presence and the activities she was organizing (see figure 2.3).

> If you look at the end of my block, here at the stop sign, it says: 'Citizen's crime watch.' We earned it, let me tell you. We [neighbors] called each other in the middle of the night. It's two o'clock in the morning and we're calling, because one of us had to be vigilant that night, and on and on and on. So thanks to the neighbors and everybody involved, you are here, on a block, that is crime-watch certified and that has changed completely for the better. Night and day.

To Alejandra's frustration, it took a lot of time before she had managed to acquire the attention of higher-ranking officials in the MPD. Eventually, the police began to consider Alejandra's initiative and determination to be a good example for other neighborhoods without a crime-watch group. Many city officials—including the district

Figure 2.3. Crime-watch meeting organized by Alejandra (not in picture), May 2015.

commissioner—came out to celebrate the crime-watch group's success with organizing local residents and collaborating with the police, and to congratulate Alejandra on her efforts, which they saw as beneficial to the whole community.

Jerry, one of the first residents of a smaller Miami neighborhood to participate in the COP program, also felt that the City of Miami did not do enough for involved citizens like himself. He also saw his interests, as a local citizen, as sometimes being at odds with the interests of law enforcement. As volunteers, Jerry explained, the COPs "can be a burden for police departments that have a different agenda. With the reporting they do, they emphasize different aspects of safety and crime than the police might want to focus on." Jerry felt that his leading role within his community was somewhat unsatisfying: "People are demanding—damned if I do, damned if I don't. But the perks are great. I easily meet with a lot of people." This was particularly useful in light of his work as a real estate developer.

While state agencies play an important role in the creation and growth of lateral surveillance programs, as does the perception of policing as an inadequate state intervention, it is just as important to recognize that public vigilance is more than a modern expression of voluntarism. In the case of the Coconut Grove crime-watch group, participants were either white or Latinx and shared stories that reproduced dominant and racist interpretations of crime. Other neighborhood crime-watch groups and captains in middle- and upper-class parts of Miami often shared very similar stories and views: that some people belong in their neighborhood, and others do not. "You know everybody, so you know when somebody does not belong," Mia, the neighborhood-watch captain in Miami Beach, told me.

> So sometimes you might think this is racist. It's not racist. This is what it is. There are people who should not be in this neighborhood. We don't want people who are driving cars at a hundred and fifty miles an hour. We don't want people with white vans and dark windows, and they're not delivering a washing machine. Or a man waiting at a bus stop where the little girls go to school. Why is he loitering there? So I will send people a reminder: this is what we're looking for. You have to be very specific, almost like teaching a child. So the more people understand it. Oh, yeah, why is there a tow truck there? Go outside, go check! So it's almost like we're encouraging people to be nosy—but we're not. What we're doing is, we're all in this together, we know the police is stretched thin, let's make it safe for us. And yes, that means that if someone here would see a Black kid walking down the street at 2 a.m., and he could be Barack Obama, people would call the police, and for a white kid, maybe not. But that's the way they think. Because he looks *different*.

Although lateral surveillance programs in theory only mobilize citizens to become the "eyes and ears" of local law enforcement, the above examples show that vigilance is about much more than that. Engaging in a wide variety of self-defense practices, surveillance, and citizen powers, vigilant citizens are often operating in a legal gray area. Yet this situation is not the result of the absence of state agencies or their unwillingness to provide security services to their constituents. In the United States, vigilantism has been a principal part of a longer institutional history of racialized violence that involves private *and* public forces (Obert 2018). Miami police officers often explained and showed that they, too, felt the need to remain vigilant during their work. Police officers wrote tickets in ways that allowed them to keep an eye on the car in front and to notice anyone approaching them. Others positioned themselves carefully when knocking at a door: not in front of the window or the door, in case the resident opened fire. Officers also said they needed to be careful and alert, both on and off duty, because people whom they have arrested in the past might recognize them and attack them.

At the same time, it is a bit of a stretch to argue that every citizen involved in lateral surveillance programs is a (potential) vigilante—public vigilance is not the same as vigilantism. Indeed, many of the vigilant citizens I met were driven by self-interest, especially in terms of their real estate investments, and so were looking to improve perceptions of safety and security in order to improve their own profits and social capital. At the end of several meetings, Alejandra joyfully exclaimed how housing prices would go up because of their collective efforts. What was noticeable was how police officers, residents, and city officials approached the communities they worked and lived in differently; these differences were, furthermore, reflective of a continuation of broader racial disparities in policing. While white and Latinx residents felt they had to "fight" for the right services and a police presence, and were rewarded in their efforts to do so, Black residents were urged to "break the silence" and disclose criminal activities to the police.

The Shop Next Door

MPD police officers and state officials frequently encourage Overtown residents to share information on criminal activities with the police. This message is communicated in many ways, including verbally during crime-watch meetings and outreach programs in the neighborhood, during which police officers actively look to interact with local residents to discuss security concerns. In March 2015, ten-year-old Marlon Eason was shot and killed in front of his house in Overtown, where he was playing with his basketball. Directly afterward, MPD police chief Rodolfo Llanes released a statement condemning the murder and expressing his difficulty in understanding any violent act that results in the loss of a child's life. In an interview with a CBS Miami reporter, Llanes explained that though he had directed police officers do to "all that is necessary to get to the bottom" of the incident, "we cannot do this alone: we need the help of the community that we have sworn to serve." He urged viewers to contact the police with whatever information they might have: "No matter how small you think it is, it may be a key part of our investigation" (Morejon 2015).

Over the next two days, police officers, supporting staff members, and residents walked through the streets of Overtown and Allapattah. Their mission was to approach and speak to anyone they encountered. Even commanding officers visited certain apartment complexes to engage in dialogue with local residents. Getting in contact with residents was sometimes difficult, as many homes have an iron fence around the property, marking the boundary between private property and public street. The officers were reluctant to venture into any front yards, to trespass on private property and knock on doors, so instead they would hit the fence with their batons and raise their voices to notify anyone inside. If a resident did come out to talk (see figure 2.1 at the beginning of this chapter), officers gave them a document detailing the incident and encouraging people to come forward with information (see figure 2.4).

As the above document indicates, the MPD sought to encourage anyone with information regarding the incident to call the Crime Stoppers phone number (the last four digits of which correspond with the word TIPS), or to visit a website where crimes can be reported anonymously. Tipsters were even eligible for a reward of up to $3,000, should their tip lead to the arrest of the killer(s). It was common in Miami at the time of my research for police departments to hand out such rewards to those who shared key information with them. Crime Stoppers, a national organization, is well known in Miami, with signs throughout the city and in Overtown. While directly connected to law enforcement agencies, the organization was specifically created to encourage local residents who might be more hesitant to contact the police to become involved in "crime fighting" by sharing knowledge. To guarantee anonymity, the organization states that they do not trace any calls and they hand out rewards in cash through a confidential tip number.

Shortly after Marlon Eason's murder, I attended the first local crime-watch meeting in Overtown. While the meeting had been scheduled before Eason's murder, MPD officers used the case to convey a sense of urgency. During the meeting, they explicitly stated that the involvement of residents was essential for law enforcement to be effective—to find and apprehend criminals and provide a sense of justice to affected families and loved ones. It was during this meeting that I met Ruth, a long-

Figure 2.4. Document distributed after the murder of Marlon Eason, March 2015. Source: Miami Police Department.

term resident of Overtown, who appeared particularly involved in the neighborhood and wanted to share her concerns with the officers present that afternoon. Like Ruth, many other participants seemed to agree, but others expressed their concerns regarding the MPD's aggressive practices. Some also complained that Miami's witness protection program was insufficient to ensure the safety of those who became police informants. Such people considered such programs crucial to overcoming the criminalization and precariousness of anyone who collaborated with law enforcement. The saying "Snitches get stitches" illustrates how those who break certain sociopolitical norms and discuss local secrets with the police invite harm (and require physical and legal protection).

A couple of weeks later, Ruth invited me to her home in Overtown. At the time, I was unfamiliar with the neighborhood and felt uncomfortable walking and biking there. Police officers and residents frequently told me that most illegal substances were sold in the area, which had acquired a reputation for being a popular local drug market. In contrast to Overtown's main corridor (NW Third Avenue), where cars are the primary mode of transport, in the streets around Ruth's apartment many residents walked and biked. Her apartment was located on the ground floor of a three-story complex. I had to drive around for a while before I was able to find a good parking spot. I called Ruth to tell her that I had arrived. My car, and certainly my appearance as a white man, attracted the attention of many residents. A group directly in front of me decided to split up when they saw me speaking on the phone. As I waited for Ruth to come out, a man walked toward me, quickly waving his arms, telling me to leave. He told me that the "shop was closed" and that I had no business there. Once she arrived, Ruth intervened, telling the man that I was her friend and insisted that she could invite whomever she wanted. She threatened to notify the police, who were parked farther down the street, with a whistle that she always carried with her. He replied that it was his right to stand in public space and that he was doing nothing wrong, but he left us alone.

Ruth explained later that the man had been trying to tell me that no drugs were being sold by her next-door neighbor at the time: his shop was closed. The residents in the apartment complex had been notified of an upcoming visit from code enforcement—city officials were coming to inspect the complex's patio, as well as Ruth's burned-out kitchen— later that morning. Ruth's neighbor, locally known as Dre, had therefore decided to temporarily suspend his business. The man outside had mistaken me for a potential customer, and he had wanted to warn me that Dre had stopped selling for the morning, or at least until code enforcement had finished their business inside the premises.

Ruth informed me of all the things she had learned about Dre's business: where he stored the drugs, at what time in the morning he cooked his meth, and who his girlfriend was—she used and sold some of his product as well. Even in the couple of hours that I spent with Ruth that first day, as soon as the shop was open again, I could hear many customers shouting his name as they walked up to the gate to complete their transaction. Ruth was frustrated by the situation. She felt as if she was being held hostage in her own home and that there was nothing she could do about it. In her words, she had to act in a way that suggested that she was "still cool" with Dre and had no intention of talking with the police. Ruth was scared of what could happen and told me that the woman who had lived in her apartment before her had had to leave because of intensifying arguments with Dre. Fearing that Dre would become violent, the previous tenant had decided to move to a different house. At the time, Ruth definitely did not have the means to afford another place and did not want her relationship with her neighbor to reach the same level of distrust and aggression. Accordingly, she was very careful when interacting with him and his friends and contacts. Her involvement in local politics as an activist—she was an active member of Miami's local BLM collective, and she also interacted with lawyers, politicians, and police officers for both personal and political reasons—amplified her concerns and complicated her relationship with her neighbor.

Ruth felt that she was increasingly subject to Dre's control, and that there was little she could do about it. Illustrative of her experience was the time that she had to store some of Dre's guns for him. Dre had told Ruth that he had gotten into a fight with his girlfriend and wanted to make sure the weapons were out of her reach if things escalated. Before Ruth could comprehend what was happening, some of Dre's illegally owned weapons were behind her couch. Ruth explained to me that it had felt as if she had become an accomplice to his illegal activities, and that she could not inform the police about anything because of this. Ruth became afraid and felt that she had to show Dre that she was not purposely looking to harm his business. She therefore spent less and less time on her front porch, where she grew tomato plants, out of fear of having to interact with him. It also became more difficult for her to invite me over, as I was clearly not a typical local resident. Ruth made several attempts to reassure Dre that she was not planning to reveal his secrets to the authorities. For example, she began to meet with Dre's girlfriend, taking her to some of the meetings that she frequented in

Overtown. Ruth hoped that his girlfriend would reassure Dre that her intentions and actions were not aimed against him.

As a final resort, Ruth decided she needed to own a handgun. She stored the .357 Magnum unloaded in a blue cotton holster under her pillow or behind her clothes in a cabinet. Although she purposefully stored the bullets separately from the handgun, out of fear that someone could break in, steal it, and use it against her or others, Ruth asserted her "right to shoot you if you come in." Ruth also assured me that should she feel compelled to take out and load the handgun, there would be no going back: she would pull the trigger. I asked her whether she had ever thought of taking weapons with her when she walked past Dre. She explained that she would not:

> No, you gotta have a concealed-weapons permit. I don't have one. You see, it's also so easy for me to be beaten up or assaulted, so my five-mile whistle and my mace is better for me. But he pushed himself on me, I told you. And I don't know why at the time I didn't think of taking pictures of him and again, writing the serial numbers of the guns.

I asked her whether she would ever consider contacting the police. She demurred:

> It would be seen like you're calling the police for help, but for what? Something someone did to you? So then you need to watch your back, because it would [be] like telling on someone, being a snitch. The police are not your friends because everybody's watching, and you might be a snitch, and you might end up dead. You don't [want] to be seen with the police or talk to them. It's unacceptable.

Ruth's experiences are illustrative of the complicated position that people find themselves in when law enforcement organizations and international anticrime organizations expect behavior that is not compliant with local norms and perceptions. The detailed information Ruth had on Dre's illegal business had clear legal implications. While it was possible that the MPD was unaware of the specifics of Dre's illegal business, it was unlikely that they needed Ruth to inform them that drugs were being produced and distributed in her neighborhood. Nevertheless, local authorities suggested in many ways that such illegal activities would only be liable for criminal prosecution if people like Ruth became vigilant citizens and shared what they knew with the MPD.

Although the anonymity of informants is stressed and witness protection programs are available, these measures did not address Ruth's daily concerns. Ruth lived under the threat of Dre every day, a fact that affected the way she interacted with him, with other residents, and with the police, and shaped her experience of living in Overtown. As such, an important part of her daily life was characterized by the danger that public vigilance campaigns posed to her. In asking her to adhere to ideals of public vigilance, international anticrime organizations such as Crime Stoppers and local police departments such as the MPD did not offer Ruth any opportunity to actually improve her daily life and safety. While Ruth supported efforts by the police and local residents to find Marlon Eason's murderer and bring them to justice, she was not sure how she could simultaneously do so without jeopardizing her own safety, in particular in terms of maintaining a good relationship with neighbors with violent tendencies. Indeed, attempts to create "good citizens" did not accommodate the local context, where state-led lateral surveillance campaigns may cause tension and uncertainty in everyday urban life.

If informing police officers is a citizen's duty, and a requirement to be part of a national political community, then Ruth was excluded. Her local environment made navigating her rights, responsibilities, and duties difficult, as national norms did not match her neighborhood reality. Ruth did not feel part of a political community of vigilant citizens, and as an activist sometimes she even opposed collaborating with state agencies and government-led gentrification. But she also did not experience herself as belonging wholly to Overtown, a place where residents distributed and used illegal substances. Dre in particular made her feel excluded. Her life as an activist provided Ruth with new contacts and relationships, an opportunity to meet likeminded people whom she could relate with.

Several days after Marlon Eason was murdered, his family members and other Overtown residents organized a vigil in a local park. Many residents attended, praying for Marlon and his mother, while lighting

Figure 2.5. Vigil after the murder of Marlon Eason, March 2015.

candles and releasing balloons into the sky. Many attending the vigil expressed both sorrow and frustration; sorrow over the fact that a ten-year-old boy had been shot, but also anger that nobody seemed to know who did it. Residents wore T-shirts that read "Stop the violence," and stated with certainty that finding and prosecuting the perpetrator would be the main way to bring justice for Marlon. But for that to happen, they reasoned, residents needed to feel empowered to "break the silence" and "take back the streets."

Ruth's strained relationship with Dre makes it difficult to generalize her experiences to other Overtown residents. Yet her case illustrates how calls to increase citizen involvement in the criminal justice system exacerbates existing vulnerabilities and inequalities. Like Ruth, many cannot live up to the expectations of "doing the right thing" and experience stress and insecurity as a result. In Ruth's view, residents of Overtown were generally suspicious and sometimes even violently opposed to those who decided to collaborate with law enforcement and anticrime organizations. As a result, she often experienced having to navigate citizenship duties and local threats on her own, in an individualized fashion.

Between Vigilance and Vigilantism

Although Santos, the security guard working on Ocean Drive in South Beach, thought of his work as "police work in a bubble," it was rather different in key ways. Four days a week, sometimes up to twelve hours a day, Santos worked at a bar, either walking around or sitting next to the entrance where he and other security guards checked customers' IDs. Santos did not enjoy his job, and frequently complained about the long hours. There was not much for him to do but to sit and wait. Only on rare occasions did he actually have to confront a customer who, for example, wore a hat inside, which was against the house rules. Indeed, Santos was mostly there to observe, to be aware of what was going on in the bar and be ready to inform the police if necessary. Like citizens involved in lateral surveillance, Santos, too, worked as the eyes and ears of law enforcement.

Santos did not like the taste of water and thus squeezed some lemonade from a small flacon into his cup. He told me he was a D-licensed security guard, which meant that he could work in positions in Florida that did not require him to be armed. In fact, it was illegal for him to carry a weapon during work: only G-licensed security guards could be hired for armed positions. But Santos told me that he did in fact come to work armed. Early on in my research, during a quiet moment, he had shown me his knife and small electroshock weapon. Most of his colleagues also knew that he carried them. What most did not know was that Santos also secretly carried a gun with him on the job. I first heard about this gun directly after Memorial Day weekend, when he told me that he had carried the gun and worn his own bulletproof vest for four days straight. Some months later, after I had gotten to know Santos better, I felt comfortable enough to begin asking more about the gun: "Did you only carry something during that weekend, or . . . ?" Santos kept his voice down, as the other security guards were sitting nearby and customers entering the bar were walking directly past us. "Nah," he answered, shaking his head and sipping from a small flask filled with water infused with flavored syrup. "How about today?" I pressed him.

SANTOS: No, not today, man. I wasn't feeling like it.
THIJS: Sooo . . . normally you do bring it with you, or no?

SANTOS: Yeah. But look at these pants, man. [He stretched his left leg out from under the barstool and twisted his foot in circles.] Too tight. They'll see it, you know. I have it with me, but not on me, if you know what I'm saying.
THIJS: But if you wear those black cargo pants?
SANTOS: Yeah. I have it there. [With his leg still out, he pointed at his ankle on the inside of his left leg.]

Whether Santos carried his gun on him at work depended on which of his pants were in the laundry. When he wore pants that were loose enough, he could attach the gun to this ankle without anyone noticing. With tight pants, he decided against having the gun on him, and instead left it in his locker inside the bar. Seemingly, the trivial matter of which pants he wore to work on a particular day determined whether Santos actually carried a gun on him or not. Having grown up in a European country where few people own guns, let alone carry one in public, I was surprised by Santos's decisions and motives. Yet we often discussed weapons, and it was clear that Santos understood them to be a primary source of personal safety. He told me about an occasion when his mother had called him after his shift had ended. She was scared at home because her alarm did not seem to be working. Santos was tired and wanted to go home. He told his mother: "Ma, you're going to be fine. There's a shotgun under your bed." Unfortunately for Santos, the weapon did not comfort her as much as it would him, and he needed to go over to fix the alarm that night.

Santos's main reason for secretly carrying a gun at the bar was that he felt uncomfortable in the environment in which he was working. He often complained about the behavior and appearance of most visitors to South Beach, primarily African Americans and Haitian Americans. Santos would sometimes insult them when he talked to me or his colleagues, but never in his interactions with the visitors themselves. He used various racial slurs, as well as called them "idiots," and "clowns," especially when he witnessed behavior that appeared illegal. When we looked out on the people in the alleyways beneath us from the bar's balcony, smoking and dealing what seemed to be marijuana, Santos stated that they "had no respect for the law." Other security guards at the bar, all white, did not comment on Santos's remarks, at least not in my presence.

For Santos, the gun on his ankle was an important asset for his work in surveillance and security. He carried it to protect himself should he feel the need. Since few people knew about the concealed weapon, Santos figured it would give him an advantage over others, an unexpected force. His secret, however, also caused tensions: it was important for him that he did not reveal it to others. Although he condemned visitors who did not follow the law, he sincerely believed that his decision to carry a gun was still lawful and considered himself to be part of a larger network of policing actors. He frequently helped MBPD police officers set up the lighting around the police towers on Ocean Drive, and discussed South Beach security concerns with them. Like many private security guards, Santos had also made several applications and enrolled in various training courses to become a police officer. During the time I knew him, however, he had not yet managed to pass any of the psychological or physical tests.

I was, however, not the only one who knew about his gun. Santos had also told Rick, the owner of Xecurity, the security company that Santos worked for. Rick, who was also an MBPD police officer, had been particularly concerned about the legal and financial risk this might pose to his company, but surprisingly he had not contested Santos's decision. Rick just told his employee that he was on his own if something were to happen. This did not bother Santos, who told me that he was more concerned with staying alive: "Shoot first, ask questions later," he joked. Although Santos knew that carrying a gun on the job was illegal, and he was concerned with keeping it a secret, he believed that the concealed weapon could be justified and legitimized by any potential circumstances in which he would reveal and possibly use his concealed weapon. Santos thereby followed the idealized notions of self-defense, vigilance, and private gun ownership, even when it was illegal for him to do so. While contesting state laws in practice, Santos acted in correspondence with his perception of the "right thing to do" given the circumstances. Santos's experience was also a very individual one, and he became a single agent in claiming what he believed to be his rights: he acted alone as he kept his gun a secret from his colleagues, while his boss distanced himself from Santos's decision and offered him no protection.

Understanding and claiming his rights to self-defense by carrying a concealed gun during work as a formally unarmed private security guard, Santos created his own room to maneuver in what he perceived to be a dangerous environment. Informed by racialized and stigmatizing stereotypes, as well as by notions of vigilant citizenship, Santos decided to illegally arm himself at the South Beach bar where he worked. Yet even as he embodied a practice of "good citizenship," Santos's primary concern, and that of his boss Rick, the MBPD police officer who owned Xecurity, was legal liability should he use the gun for the "wrong" reasons; that is, reasons that could not legitimize his actions in a court of law.

Santos's racialized understandings and aggressive tactics show how vigilance is a product of a longer institutional history of racialized violence and white vigilantism, involving both public and private actors. Jonathan Obert (2018) shows that throughout history, state and nonstate actors "effectively coordinate violence independently but in concert with one another" (2018: 6). While vigilantism initially had a local and sporadic character, organized around slave control, Obert discusses how patterns of vigilantism eventually became part of day-to-day forms of political authority and white control. Public vigilance and lateral surveillance, in other words, is about more than working as the "eyes and ears" of law enforcement. Citizens engage in a wide variety of self-defense and policing practices, surveillance, and citizen powers. Obert explains that though these actors technically operate in a legal gray zone, their vigilance and vigilantism has been supported, condoned, and encouraged by the apparatus of government. This makes lateral surveillance, and public vigilance more broadly, part of a form of racialized violence that is produced and perpetuated by the state itself.

Beyond Lateral Surveillance

State agencies frame the act of observing as an essential duty for membership of a political community of vigilant citizens. Ruth's case in particular shows how this mobilization of local residents in programs of lateral surveillance can create tensions in terms of citizens' sense of belonging to a political community. They can also cultivate feelings of suspicion, fear, and individualization—feelings that have become embedded in cultural notions of citizenship in the United States. The examples of lateral surveillance provided in this chapter are just a small selection of the various ways in which residents are taught and enabled to surveil one another. Fingerprinting your children—as recommended by the FBI and local child safety organizations—might increase the chances of recovering your child if she were to go missing. But how might this affect relationships within a family or community, and how does it shape the child's perception of the world she lives in?

Do the right thing refers to not only the MPD program but also Spike Lee's 1989 film, which he wrote, produced, and directed. This film explores the racial tensions in a Brooklyn neighborhood in the aftermath of a police killing of a Black man. The major question it raises is whether the protagonist, a Black man, "does the right thing" when, in reacting to that killing, he helps incite a riot that nearly destroys a local white-owned business. Lee complicates that question for his audience by pitting two views of violence vis-à-vis justice, one from Martin Luther King, Jr., the other from Malcom X, at the end of the film. He has also remarked that it is mostly white viewers who wonder whether the main character actually does the right thing—Black viewers seem to know the answer already.[2] The perpetual denial of racial injustice on the part of white citizens, their unwillingness to acknowledge and understand racism, is part of the reason why Lee dedicated the film to the families of six victims of both police brutality and racial violence.

In this chapter, I try to show how law enforcement agencies use the same framework of "doing the right thing" to build a community of vigilant citizens. Neighborhood-watch groups in particular thrive on notions of being vigilant, as an indication of their proactive and good citizenship. Police officers and local residents consider lateral surveillance key for public safety, and articulations of being vigilant appear dominant in what it means to "do the right thing." In practice, however, much of these collaborations and actions that blur the boundaries between the police and citizens sustain and intensify racial disparities already seen in everyday policing. Participants in neighborhood watches, and members who feel part of a collective of vigilant citizens more generally, were often driven by racialized fears and insecurity. Black Miamians are seen and policed differently through not only a lens of normative whiteness but also the dominant understanding of what "doing the right thing" means (namely, that acting so will result in a just outcome, in an accurate assessment of guilt and innocence). It is the police message that drug dealer Dre, whose business made the lives of his neighbors more stressful, will never be arrested unless a neighbor, like Ruth, actively cooperates with the MPD. This is why police officers encourage and sometimes press residents to collaborate and share information with them. After the murder of Marlon Eason, police officers urged local residents to "break the silence" and disclose any information they had to Crime Stoppers. Informants could remain anonymous and would receive financial compensation for their act of "good citizenship"—the adult version of the free pizza offered by the DTRT campaign. Yet local residents stressed the need to create conditions in which "snitches" no longer had to fear for their safety. Even as working together with local law enforcement authorities is framed as an essential citizenship duty, it is impossible to avoid the tensions and feelings of alienation that often emerge at a local level.

Interestingly, the examples of lateral surveillance discussed in this chapter—from Paco's COP group, to Alejandra's neighborhood-watch initiative, and Ruth's and Santos's individualized experiences—all relate to private gun ownership. The lived experiences and examples of vigilant citizenship discussed in this chapter situate lateral surveillance programs within broader forms of violent and racialized policing. Mobilized as policing actors, citizens, too, observe, register, and act upon their surroundings through notions of normative whiteness. To look beyond lateral surveillance, to unpack the romanticized presentation of citizens as the "eyes and ears" of state agencies, is to acknowledge that vigilance and vigilantism exist on the same continuum. Both are rooted in a system of white supremacy that transgresses institutional—and legal—boundaries. Following where these experiences and actions of vigilant citizenship have taken us, the next chapter delves deeper into the everyday realities of self-defense laws and private gun ownership.

Figure 3.1. Street in the neighborhood where Olaf and I lived in 2015, February 2015.

3

Guns for the Good Guys

Olaf, a white American man in his late twenties, was a musician, and my roommate during my fieldwork in Miami. Together with his girlfriend, he lived just north of Wynwood and had been looking for a roommate online. Olaf was happy with my reply, as he had been receiving "a lot of crazy and weird emails." A couple of days after I arrived in Miami, Olaf showed me the shotgun he owned. He kept the Remington 12-gauge pump-action shotgun stored in its original carton under the king-size bed he and his girlfriend slept in. Olaf also kept it loaded. The only thing you had to do was load the shell into the chamber by pumping the handle on the bottom. Olaf was not particularly fond of guns or weapons in general for that matter. However, he told me, he had chosen to buy and own a shotgun because of the sound, the famous "click-clack" that you hear when you load a shell into the chamber. He believed that the sound alone would be enough to scare off any perceived threats, so he would not actually have to shoot anyone.

One night, Olaf came home late and took out the garbage to be collected the next morning. He opened the electric fence in our front yard and drove the Mini Cooper his girlfriend had recently bought onto the street to make room for the garbage bin to be able to be rolled through. Olaf parked the car in the middle of the street and walked back toward the house to grab the garbage bin, leaving the engine running. The moment he turned his back, a man quickly walked over to the Mini, entered it, and began to drive away with the door still open. Olaf ran toward his girlfriend's car, shouted, and was able to pull the driver by his leg, but immediately let him go. He realized there was no way of knowing whether the man was armed, and the car was not worth risking physical injury, let alone death. As he saw the car making a turn toward the main road, a white van that had been parked across the intersection also took off in the same direction as the Mini.

Olaf stormed back into the house, called 911, and knocked repeatedly on my door. We waited for the police together as he told me what had happened. The car was worth a lot of money, and his relationship with his girlfriend was already strained. A stolen Mini was not going to make things any better soon. It was a long and frustrating night for my roommate. One of the MPD officers who had responded to his call leaned back against his police car and rested his hands on his belt. He told Olaf that either they would find the car quickly or it was unlikely that it would ever be recovered. "What can I say? It's Miami, man," the police officer explained to Olaf. By this, he meant to say that such incidents "just happened" in the city, and that there was only so much anyone could do about it. It was a risk you had to accept when living there. Olaf was also disappointed by the response of our neighbors, none of whom seemed to care much about what had happened either. Together with the lackluster performance of the MPD, this made him feel suddenly uncomfortable about living in the neighborhood. He recalled how his family, who lived in Miami Beach, had warned him about moving to this part of Miami. Had it been a mistake to ignore their advice?

Most of Olaf's friends and family members owned and carried a gun. After hearing about the incident with the Mini, Olaf's personal trainer began to carry his loaded handgun at the top of his equipment bag when he came to our house. Some of Olaf's friends told him that they would have shot the man for sure. Olaf, however, told me that he was happy that he had not been carrying a gun at the time—he was afraid that he would have actually shot him and doubted whether it was worth hurting or even killing someone over a car. The law entitled Olaf to own and use a gun. Because private gun ownership is legal in Miami—as in all of the United States—Olaf could purchase and own a shotgun to protect us and his belongings in and directly around the house. The law allowed him to use or threaten to use lethal force when faced with imminent danger. His shotgun transformed my roommate into a "first responder": Olaf would not be forced to wait for the MPD to come to his aid, he could intervene in a dangerous situation himself. Yet Olaf wondered when and how he could use the weapon in a way that was both ethically and legally justifiable.

In the United States, private gun ownership is grounded in the Second Amendment of the Constitution, and it has been expanded in some states by so-called castle-doctrine legislation and stand-your-ground laws (Boots et al. 2009). When it comes to private gun ownership, the National Rifle Association (NRA) successfully lobbied to expand self-defense legislation throughout the United States that "redefines and expands the locations and situations when an individual may use force to defend their person or property without having any duty to retreat" (Boots et al. 2009: 516). These statutes justify self-defense even outside the home, the traditional "castle" where private gun ownership was originally legalized, providing additional legal grounds to justify the use of lethal force. An analysis of historical and contemporary policies in the United States indicates that "the white majority has often used gun regulation as a tool to keep firearms out of the hands of politically unpopular groups that it deemed to be too dangerous" (Gulasekaram 2010: 1542).

Private gun ownership can be understood as not so much an easily claimed universal right but an unevenly distributed privilege that paradoxically has become a defining aspect of citizenship status, creating second-class citizens who are unable to access these rights. Traditionally, those who were not covered by the Second Amendment were enslaved people, immigrants, and specific racial and ethnic groups. Much like police gun violence, private gun ownership is rooted in American racism and settler colonialism, and both have "normalized racialized violence and affinity for firearms in U.S. society" (Dunbar-Ortiz 2018: 39). Today, it is illegal for Florida residents with a registered felony to own a gun (or to vote), though they may seek to have their gun rights reinstated through a complicated and often unsuccessful legal procedure. Considering the disproportionate incarceration rates for African Americans and Latinx in comparison to white people in the United States, exclusion from gun ownership based on felony convictions is therefore strongly linked to race (e.g., Wacquant 2001).

This means that guns are given a different meaning and status depending on whose hands they are in: some guns are perceived as contributing to public safety, others are considered to be a threat to it. Legitimate gun use is in part dependent on the legality of gun ownership. Stolen guns become a threat because they are no longer "legal." For example, the US Department of Justice (DOJ) encourages citizens to keep a record of their personal firearms, reasoning that if a gun is stolen, it is more easily recovered when characteristics such as model, manufacturer, and serial number are known. The DOJ has therefore distributed a document that gun owners can voluntarily use to keep track of their firearms, because "a stolen gun threatens everyone" (US Department of Justice, 2013). Although guns are both widely available and subject to decreasing regulation, this gesture illustrates that the authorities are concerned about illegal gun ownership, which in their view constitutes a direct threat to public safety.

At the same time, guns are considered essential for anyone involved in policing—not just police officers. The private security industry, for instance, differentiates between "D" and "G" licenses; the latter allows a private security guard to legally carry a firearm while at work. G-licensed security guards receive a higher salary, which is an incentive for aspiring security guards to learn how to use a gun. Many people I met in the course of this research owned a gun. They stored them underneath their bed, hidden behind their underwear, under their pillow, or simply left them on their nightstand. This chapter explores what guns mean in terms of how different Miami residents can enact and experience vigilant citizenship.

Among Sheep and Wolves

Guns are perhaps both the most common and the most contested security object in the United States. Nationally, there are over three hundred companies involved in the business of small arms production, and approximately 393 million privately owned guns are distributed over 40 percent of US households.[1] Opinions on private gun ownership divide the nation and correlate with political preferences: states with the most gun owners vote Republican, and states with the fewest vote Democrat. There is, however, little reliable and up-to-date statistical information available regarding private gun ownership. For political and economic reasons, the NRA has managed to keep research on gun ownership and gun violence to a minimum and off the political agenda. According to the RAND Corporation, a nonprofit organization and think tank, about one-third of Florida's adult population owns one or more firearms, which is around the national average. In 2019, the National Center for Health Statistics reported that Florida's firearm death rate (the number of gun-related deaths per hundred thousand residents) was 12.9, also around the national average and the equivalent of 2,945 gun-related deaths a year.[2]

The Second Amendment protects private gun ownership at the national scale, but within the parameters set by the Constitution, individual states can introduce specific legislation and regulation that applies to their geographical territories. Florida has relatively lax gun regulations. Any official resident of the state who is over the age of twenty-one can legally purchase a handgun after completing a standard criminal history check and a seventy-two-hour waiting period. In 1986, Florida introduced the "shall-issue" legislation, which basically entitles every resident that meets the basic criteria to receive a license to carry. The legislation replaced previous regulations that required applicants to convince state officials of their need for such a license (Carlson 2015). With this basic permit, it is legal to carry a gun inside the home, and also—when the gun is "securely encased"—in a private vehicle. Although I heard different interpretations of what "securely encased" entails in practice, the general consensus seemed to be that the gun should not be easily accessible, with its encasement preventing anyone from grabbing and using the weapon quickly. An additional concealed-carry license, however, allows citizens to move through public space while carrying a weapon as long as it is not directly visible to others. Many who carry their weapons in public attach a small holster to their belt and conceal the gun with a large shirt.

Olaf had bought his shotgun some years earlier in a shop on the outskirts of Wynwood. I visited the store a couple of times and eventually became acquainted with Alex, the gun store manager. In addition to chatting with Alex, I also talked to police officers and customers in the store about recent shootings, crime, and security in Miami, and of course private gun ownership. Rico, the MPD police officer whom I sometimes joined on patrol, also frequented the same store. As we were waiting one time for a call to come in, he and his colleagues began to discuss the body armor that another officer had just bought: it was smaller, lighter, and therefore easier to wear during foot chases or fist fights, while still protecting the officer's vital organs. As he tried it on and checked out his reflection in the tinted window of his car, Rico stated that he would certainly pick up the same vest for himself soon.

During one visit to the store, I found Alex cleaning a Glock handgun behind the counter. He began explaining to me why gun owners were so important for public safety. Using the analogy of dogs, wolves, sheep, and sheepdogs, the manager differentiated between individual roles in society. Dogs were the police officers who tried to stop the wolves, that is, the criminals. These wolves targeted innocent sheep: peaceful but ignorant citizens. According to Alex, sheep lived their lives blind to the crime happening around them. Confronted with crime or violence, they were always surprised to hear of such practices to begin with. Sheep were not necessarily bad in his view, but they were relatively useless to society as they did nothing to prevent illegal behavior from occurring and contributed nothing to actually improving the safety of the larger community. Sometimes, Alex told me, it was even because of the sheep's ignorance that criminals got away with crimes unpunished.

Alex explained that guns transformed individuals from ignorant civilians into policing actors who actually contributed to the safety of the communities around them. A main characteristic of sheep was that they did not own a gun or were for various reasons incapable of using one. Guns were the key difference between sheep and sheepdogs, the term he used to describe private gun owners. According to Alex, legal private gun owners could assist police officers who are unable to be everywhere at the same time. Sheepdogs could therefore respond before the actual dogs arrived, to protect the sheep from the wolves. Alex said that he was much more relaxed knowing that his wife, who was out shopping, was protected by people with guns who could intervene if she found herself in trouble. "Although we look like sheep," Alex said, "we can still fight like dogs." Such narratives describe private gun ownership as not only a right but also responsibility, sometimes even a troubling and burdensome duty. The right to bear arms has become entangled with idealized notions of citizenship, in particular the vigilant type; private gun ownership is valued, and people who own guns are perceived as contributing more to the (political) communities of which they are a part. Current laws make the use of a lethal weapon for the protection of persons or property legal, and in combination with certain normative frameworks they even encourage such behavior.

I asked Alex if I should buy a shotgun, since many—not just Olaf—had advised me to because of the sound it makes and its effect as a deterrent. Alex responded by saying that the sound is just an incentive to the burglar to shoot first, so he rather recommended the AR-15. Plus, he added, a shotgun has a much smaller range than many movies would have you believe. The AR-15, with its penetrating high-impact bullets and high-capacity magazines would "give you the perfect option to protect your castle." Furthermore, since I was unfamiliar with guns in general, he advised me to start with a handgun first, then an AR-15 machine gun, after which I could later add a shotgun to complete my arsenal.

Once we were finished talking, Alex walked away to help a customer and I read the back of his polo shirt: "Guns for the good guys." Echoing the message on his shirt, politicians and supporters of the right to bear arms use explanations and analogies very similar to Alex's story of dogs, wolves, sheep, and sheepdogs to explain why and how private gun ownership is important for public safety. As responses to many recent mass shootings and violence in the United States indicate, this seems like the go-to argument for anyone who thinks that "more guns" is the answer. According to this perspective, the only solution to the bad guys with guns is to arm more good guys with guns.

Such typologies are not exclusive to the staff of this particular store in Wynwood but are indicative of how policing actors identify and treat citizens more broadly. In his famous article, John van Maanen (1978) analyzes how police officers view citizens and make a tripartite distinction between the categories of "suspicious persons," "assholes," and "know nothings." The "asshole," most importantly, "can be seen as a sort of reified other, representing all those persons who would question, limit, or otherwise attempt to control the police" (1978: 323). Such oversimplified and stigmatizing categorizations shape and justify the way policing actors—whether they are police officers or armed citizens—expect, think, feel, and behave in public. In doing so, policing actors continue to reify classifications of who they believe are similar to themselves, who are different, and who are a threat (van Maanen 1978).

The NRA in particular plays an important role in shaping public policies regarding guns, making the weapon meaningful in the hands of both citizens and police officers alike. Indeed, guns and policing are entangled in a broader agenda of law and order. And while law enforcement agencies have been in favor of gun control policies in the past, recent studies suggest that most officers support private gun ownership—perhaps surprisingly, considering that it could also make their own work more dangerous. Here, the NRA popularized the notion that the police need guns in their daily work, and that carrying a weapon (whether by police officer or civilian), is an act of good citizenship (Carlson 2014; 2015; 2020). These policies in turn are used to distinguish between "legitimate" and "criminal" violence, which generally serves to perpetuate and intensify systemic violence and racial inequality (Carlson 2014; 2015; 2020).

Private gun ownership, like vigilance, is not so much about responding to security needs left by an absent or weak police force; rather, it is intrinsic to the workings of a nation-state and therefore an extension of state violence. In 2020, in the context of BLM protests, police brutality, and the COVID-19 pandemic, armed citizens took to the streets in Kenosha, Wisconsin, Washington, DC, and various other cities across the United States to "maintain order." Police officers thanked these groups for providing protection during times of civil unrest. Supported and endorsed by police officers, journalists, and politicians, such displays of force, as well as practices of vigilant citizenship, laid bare how "the distinctions between vigilantism and lawful arrest and punishment have always been murky" (Obert 2020). Such acts of vigilantism, in turn, speak to what scholars have called the "militarization of urban life": "the idea that the internal geographies of the US are the sites of state-backed wars against racialized and biopolitically disposable others as much as external actors" (Graham 2012: 140). Analyzing how military and security complexes increasingly transform urban life, Stephen Graham (2012) explains that the logics found in international warfare are equally applied to urban space. Private gun ownership does not just arm and enable white supremacists: it is inherently connected to the racist logics and systemic violence that underlies policing, involving both private and public actors. These vigilante groups, as Mark Estes, a professor of American Studies, also states in an interview, actually uphold the original and historical intent of the Second Amendment (Mathias 2020). How and when private gun ownership translates to everyday policing is, however, neither unilinear nor universal, but is informed by a politics of difference.

Differentiated Gun Ownership

Alex and other customers at the gun store told me stories of people they knew who had defended themselves against intruders, and showed me videos of shootings. For them, private gun ownership was also related to other attributes of good citizenship, such as home ownership. One police officer who frequented the gun store glowed with pride as he showed me a picture of his thirteen-year-old daughter practicing with a shotgun. To him and others, teaching his kid to shoot was indicative of good fatherhood. Other customers told me that they had bought a handgun exactly because they had gone from being a tenant to a homeowner. They saw this status as involving additional responsibilities, and some figured that a gun would allow them to protect their investment. It is, however, too much of a stretch to argue that such normative ideals by themselves force people either to buy a gun or to live with the stigma of being a sheep. There are many who escape this binary, for example by living comfortably without a gun, or by actively opposing gun legislation as part of a collectivity with a shared interest in restricting gun ownership. The point here is therefore not to argue that there is no way of escaping the glorification of private gun ownership in everyday life, but to suggest that these dominant narratives inform concrete acts and experiences of citizenship.

On one of my visits to the gun store in Wynwood, I read the sign on the front door more carefully. It indicated the kind of potential customers who were welcome in the store and those who were not. As figure 3.2 shows, potential customers who wore their pants so low that their underwear was visible were told not to come in. I asked Alex about the sign, and he told me that he preferred that anyone entering the store should maintain a certain appearance. In his words, this was no more than a matter of respect and courtesy. The sign suggested that people who show no "decency" for others—by showing their underwear—were perhaps also not the ideal type of gun owner. Although Alex had a different explanation, to me this dress code was clearly addressed at young African Americans, suggesting vividly how private gun ownership is used to exclude certain population groups based on racialized stereotypes (Gulasekaram 2010).

A couple of blocks south of the Wynwood gun store was the Overtown barbershop where Marcus walked around the chair that his cus-

Figure 3.2. Sign on the front door of a gun store in Wynwood, March 2015.

tomers sat in. His jeans hung loosely around his upper legs, his colorful underwear clearly showing underneath his white T-shirt. Marcus told me how much he valued his right to own and carry a gun, because it enabled him to protect himself, his wife and child, and even me sitting inside his barbershop. While the gun store sign did not make it illegal or impossible for Marcus to purchase and own a gun, it suggested that at least some people questioned whether and how his gun contributed to public safety. It indicated that there was a difference between Marcus's gun and Olaf's gun.

To understand how private gun ownership creates and perpetuates differentiated citizenship, it is useful to distinguish between "hard" and "soft" laws (von Benda-Beckmann et al. 2009). Hard laws refer to the actual written laws used in a court of law. These laws, for example, determine the necessary conditions for private gun ownership to be legal, and thus they differentiate between citizens who are eligible to own a gun and those who are not. Citizens who can pass the background check performed by a gun salesman can therefore buy a gun at a store. Although soft laws cannot define a particular form of private gun ownership as illegal, they do reflect broader interpretations of how and when guns actually contribute to public safety. More specifically, soft laws refer to "governance through peer review, consultation, peer pressure, shaming and the creation of non-binding guidelines and recommendations" (von Benda-Beckmann et al. 2009: 9). Although hard laws dictate that citizens who meet the legal criteria are eligible to buy and own a gun, soft laws tell a different story: some guns contribute to public safety, and others do not; some gun owners are legitimate sheepdogs, others are more likely to be wolves.

Racialized understandings of how guns contribute to public safety also exist on a larger scale, when they are institutionalized through public policy and state practices. For example, Miami police departments and city officials have organized numerous gun-buyback programs that take place several times throughout the year. These programs are seen as a way to curb gun violence and mass shootings in the United States, and they are even supported by scholars such as Nancy Scheper-Hughes, who see them as a response to the "militarization of everyday life in countries accustomed to war," in which "war crimes gradually seep into civilian life" (2014: 8).

In March 2016, a gun-buyback event took place at a missionary church in Liberty City, a neighborhood in Miami with a reputation for having a high crime rate, similar to Overtown. NBC Miami reporters were present during the event and claimed it to have been a huge success: "more than a hundred guns now off the streets and out of the hands of anyone who could be dangerous," the anchorman summarized (Glover, 2016). In return for their guns, residents received gift cards of $50 to $200, depending on the kind of weapon they had handed in. The program did not require anyone to officially register or show identification: guns could be handed in anonymously and no police officer would ask any questions. Thomas Regalado, the mayor of Miami at the time, was present during the Liberty City gun buyback and asserted that the bottom line of the event was that the parties involved had managed to get more than one hundred guns off the city's streets.

The gun-buyback programs that took place during my fieldwork were, however, primarily organized in neighborhoods known for their high crime rate. State agencies did not define private gun ownership per se to be problematic and dangerous, but they did consider stolen, illegal, and unwanted guns to be a threat to public safety. The organizers of the gun-buyback programs reasoned that these guns were primarily in the hands of Latinx and African American residents living in infamous Miami neighborhoods. Similarly, and related to the previous chapter, stakeholders also used the program to "build relationships." According to activists and police officers, these relationships were necessary to persuade residents to "speak up," claiming that there "was no such thing as snitching" when it came to gun violence (Glover 2016).

The gun-buyback programs that I observed not only suggested a selective and racialized understanding of the dangers of private gun ownership; they were also indicative of how responsibility for public safety is distributed in larger society. In Florida, at the time of my research, private gun ownership was legal for a person when basic criteria (including a minimum age of twenty-one, residency, and passing an instantaneous background check) are met. Technically speaking, there is no requirement of the applicant to demonstrate "good cause," and authorities are expected to issue a gun license. In other words, if the goal was to reduce "unwanted guns," state agencies could also have imposed stricter gun laws. Yet they relied on soft laws, such as nonbinding guidelines and recommendations, to make citizens responsible for bringing in the guns themselves. Since the NRA lobby made it difficult, if not impossible, for politicians to pass stricter gun laws, local police departments had few alternative strategies. Similarly, buyback programs for toy guns across the United States offer children nonviolent toys in return for their pistols and rifles. These programs are illustrative of the extent to which the consumers of security products and violent toys are held responsible for public safety, rather than the state in terms of regulating the market for such objects. Instead of changing private gun laws, state agencies ask residents of predominantly Black neighborhoods, such as Liberty City and Overtown, to give up their right to self-defense, a right that has become central to acts and experiences of citizenship, legal or illegal.

A Legal Shot?

As I accompanied Rico on a ride-along during one of his patrols, the MPD officer received a request from the police dispatcher. A 911 call had come in from a security guard who felt unable to deal with an intoxicated man harassing visitors in a park in Downtown Miami. Rico, another MPD officer, and I found the drunken man stumbling around a bench by a footpath overlooking the ocean, sipping from a bottle. He was white, wearing jeans and a gray T-shirt, and some of his belongings were scattered in the grass around him. Rico greeted him and asked him politely to collect his things and leave the park. The man appeared unresponsive to Rico's requests, but grabbed a rubber hammer from his backpack and began to twirl around with it in a slow and uncontrolled manner. The three of us stood still as Rico repeated his request a few more times. I did not feel threatened by the man's behavior, and neither of the police officers seemed very impressed. Still, the man was carrying a rubber hammer, an object that could be classified as a weapon. He was also trespassing on private property, publicly intoxicated, and was ignoring direct instructions issued by two police officers. Rico wondered aloud, "Can I shoot him?"

It was clear to me that Rico was not actually considering taking out his handgun and firing it, potentially injuring or killing the drunken man. Rather, and in light of recent debates around police brutality, Rico was trying to figure out what was still legal in the given context. His question, and his interpretation of the scene, were motivated by a desire to understand the physical and emotional conditions that constituted a legitimate reason to shoot, a reason that could hold up in court. Carefully observing the man, who had begun to pack up his belongings, the two police officers concluded that yes, Rico could have shot the man without being found guilty in a court of law. Eventually, the man left the park and the officers' presence was required elsewhere: three skateboarding teenagers were flouting the park rules and ignoring the security guard's requests to leave.

Rico sought to read the threat of violence in terms of not only the actual risk of physical harm but also broader and shared understandings of the law, the latter involving working out what constituted a weapon, legally speaking, and what rules and laws the intoxicated man was breaking. He drew on his interpretations of the law to understand the parameters of his own agency or his room to maneuver, which in this case included exploring the possibility of shooting a man without being prosecuted or found guilty in a court of law. While we might of course expect a law enforcement officer to have an above-average awareness of what constitutes the legal use of force, Rico's immediate, explicit framing of the encounter in legal terms was striking.

On several other occasions, Rico explained to me what he believed was the appropriate and justified use of force for a police officer. For example, shortly after we left the park, Rico showed me a video of the police killing of James Bushey in Texas in 2015. The video, recorded by the body cameras of the officers, shows how the officers found Bushey in the bathroom of a local Applebee's restaurant. The officers suspected that Bushey had stolen alcohol and escorted him outside to make the arrest. Once outside, Bushey drew what appeared to be a weapon, turned around, and aimed the object at the officers, who immediately responded by shooting Bushey and killing him. Afterward, investigators determined that Bushey's weapon was a BB gun, and media sources suggested that Bushey—who was divorced and had recently been fired from his job—had deliberately put his own life at risk by aiming the gun at the officers. Officer Rico agreed with the decision to not prosecute the officers and considered the use of force legitimate. Indeed, based on the video, it seems reasonable to believe that both officers acted out of fear for their own lives, and that the use of lethal force seemed necessary.

Although legality is often a performance and a facade for the administration of violence and coercion by the police, it remains a popular framework for interpreting and evaluating police (gun) violence. "One of the central assumptions made about 'modern' policing," Mark Neocleous begins his chapter on law and order, "is that it is concerned first and foremost with law" (2000: 92). Challenging the idea that policing only involves responding to crime and maintaining a rule of law, Neocleous argues that "despite the immensely complex legal relation surrounding the police (brought about in part by a hegemonic liberalism as the core ideology of bourgeois society), the police function should be seen through the lens of administration as much as law" (2000: 95). While police officers are expected to deter and respond to a number of crimes by enforcing the law, their work is an "exercise of administrative power as much as anything else" (2000: 94). In addition, what "legal" entails in practice can be extended by the police itself—because law is a product of state agencies and flexible enough to uphold the idea of the legality of police work. Imagined as a neutral and independent instrument, capable of providing justice, the law is still considered to be a meaningful and useful framework for both policing actors and policed citizens to interpret and evaluate policing—a point that I expand on in the next chapter.

The understanding that lethal force is legal for those defending themselves from a direct threat of grave bodily harm or death can lead to a seemingly warped logic of gun use. Police officers, private security guards, and private gun owners told me that where on the body you shot an attacker would be read as legal evidence of the measure of threat you were facing. An MPD police instructor told me that if he did not aim and fire at the torso of someone posing a threat, he would render himself liable to prosecution. "Shooting at the arms or legs could be a reason for the victim to sue me for illegal dismemberment," the instructor explained. After all, he reasoned, if there were truly an imminent threat, why would you aim for the limbs to begin with? A judge and jury might make the same assessment.

Maurice Punch (2011) discusses the policy for police officers to "shoot to stop," which is different from "shoot to kill." Police officers are taught to aim at the torso, and "not to try to 'shoot to wound,' because hitting the suspect is too uncertain and it is too risky as the suspect can continue the threatening behavior even when seriously wounded" (2011: 9). Although this may very likely result in the suspect's death, the intention to kill is officially not the main reason why police officers shoot. Punch (2011) identifies this shift in shooting policies—from "shoot to prevent" to "shoot to kill"—as being embedded in an "informal cop code" that advises officers never to draw a weapon unless they have the intention of taking a life.

During an MPD training course I attended, instructors discussed the case of a shooting. The father of one recruit—also a police officer—had been involved in the shooting of a homeless man who had assaulted another homeless man. In his hand, the former had held a Walkman, which the officers, including the recruit's father, had mistaken for a pistol. They shot him in the leg. To cover up their error, they had placed a gun on the scene; this was eventually found out and resulted in the suspension of and legal complications for the officers. Nevertheless, the question that the instructors and recruits were discussing was whether it had been a good shot. "No, because he missed him—he shot him in his leg," one recruit answered, and the others started to laugh. The question here was, however, related to whether the shot had been justified (was it a "good" use of force?), and the consensus was that it had in fact been a good shot, because the officers had believed a person's life was in danger.

Recent discussions of police violence point to the issue of qualified immunity: a juridical doctrine that shields all law enforcement officers from being held personally liable for actions performed during their duty. Yet these discussions of a legal shot suggest these officers do not seem to operate from the assumption that they can use lethal force with impunity—that to them, there is a difference between a "good" and a "bad" shot. Their actions, and in particular their use of the police handgun, tend to be calibrated around these distinctions. These act of framing the legitimate use of force in legal terms, as a question of what constitutes a *legal shot*, extended beyond the work of police officers. Although federal and state laws recognize self-defense as legal, the conditions that justify firing a gun remain subject to judicial interpretation. Legal professionals and state agencies that suggest that there is a fine line between murder and self-defense reinforce this ambiguity. For example, the gun store in Wynwood distributed information from US LawShield, a national organization that aims to educate its "members in self-defense law; empower them to handle critical, life-threatening situations with confidence; and protect them from potential injustices in the legal system after acts of self-defense" (US LawShield 2018). Shared understandings of the law shape how guns are used in practice, often more than ethical and social concerns regarding whether, how, and when private gun ownership actually contributes to public safety.

Several booklets on display in the gun store suggested that gun owners need to have a thorough understanding of the self-defense legislation to justify their use of a gun. While the organizations that distribute these booklets emphasize these uncertainties to sell the services they offer, it is indicative of a broader understanding that knowledge of the law and access to legal services are crucial to prevent being sued by other parties. The first page in "a free special report" by US LawShield, for example, had a space reserved for the emergency phone number of a lawyer. Such imaginaries of legality built around private gun ownership focus on navigating legal accountability and justifying self-defense in court, and on the notion that knowledge of the law is the best way to prevent murder. Murder as a legal classification, that is, not necessarily in terms of how a death might be framed in the experience of ordinary people.

Such entanglements between legality and legitimacy in gun violence are embedded not only in everyday police practices but also popular culture. In "Volcano" (1997) of the animated satirical sitcom *South Park*, two hunters are not allowed to hunt animals. To circumvent these regulations, whenever they see an animal they shout, "It's coming right for us!" before shooting it, so that they can legitimize the shooting as a form of self-defense and thus justifiable by law. Similarly, Ruth and Santos, who both owned and sometimes carried a gun, also imagined that if ever they were to pull out their gun, they would be sure to fire it. They both believed that if they merely pulled out the gun, then they would need to explain why they had threatened someone with it in the first place, while shooting would provide a legal justification—it was self-defense. In other words, such shared understandings of the law—whether fully accurate or misreadings of jurisprudence—can make it more likely that guns will actually be used lethally in practice.

Everyday (Police) Gun Violence

Outside of everyday policing encounters, the gun is central to police training and practice. In Miami, police recruits and officers train in Meggitt simulations, which is an immersive and virtual training system for law enforcement. Entering a dark room, participants stand in front of a large screen onto which multiple scenes are projected, with the instructor controlling how different scenes will play out. During one scene, you play a police officer who has just pulled over a driver going over the speed limit. It is up to the participant how to approach the driver: What do you ask him? How do you position yourself? Where do you keep your hands? Depending on these decisions, the instructor decides what happens next: Will the driver pull out a knife from the glove compartment? Will he comply? Will he start running?

Others, including former police officers and police instructors, were critical of the Meggitt system, because it centers on the question of when to shoot and when to use a nonlethal weapon or verbal commands. One former officer who became an instructor at a private security company asked me whether I had experienced the program myself. He explained that police officers are taught to identify certain "markers" that legitimize the use of force. In other words, what needs to happen for a police officer to use a gun. The former instructor told me that he considered police training's focus on the gun to be problematic and, in his eyes, one of the reasons why police gun violence has become everyday practice.

Researching police brutality in Chicago, Laurence Ralph (2020) discusses the so-called use-of-force continuum—the guidelines that police officers are supposed to follow when determining how much force they can use. "Police officers," Ralph writes, "are *required* to make their way through all reasonable alternatives before deploying force" (2020: xxi; original emphasis). Accordingly, police officers draw on the use-of-force continuum to navigate between the various means at their disposal. In doing so, they are "permitted to always be one step ahead" (2020: xxi). Ralph points out that in practice, however, police officers escalate their use of force based on racist interpretations of what actually constitutes a threat. While the continuum in theory should protect citizens from a disproportionate use of force, it becomes a guideline to legalize every step of police brutality.

During my first ride-along with MBPD police officer Alf, an emergency call came in as we were driving over the causeway, making our way back to Miami Beach. Alf immediately turned on the sirens and alarm lights, and I heard how the Ford's engine was pushed to maximum as we accelerated toward an intersection. There I saw a white car being followed by several police cars, one of them driven by Alf's lieutenant, who had notified all the other patrol officers that the driver in front of him had ignored the lieutenant's signal for the driver to pull over. Passing through a red light, we joined the group of police cars, and after a short chase, the white car pulled over and five police cars stopped several meters behind it. Surrounded by his colleagues, Alf pulled out his handgun, jumped out of the vehicle, and aimed the gun at the white car, which was illuminated by the bright searchlights on top of the police cars. One of the men inside the white car opened the door, to which the police lieutenant responded by shouting, "Stay in the car!" With guns drawn, several police officers approached the white car and after a short exchange learned that the four men inside were Brazilian, and that they had only been trying to get out of the way when the lieutenant had used his "stop" sign to indicate for them to pull over; according to them, this is what you do in Brazil. After their IDs had been checked and returned, the officers left the scene.

When Alf returned to his police car, he found me hiding underneath the dashboard, still somewhat overwhelmed by the police response and the threat of gun violence. I slowly climbed back into my seat. While I never witnessed police officers firing their weapons, this encounter was one of many in which police officers drew their handguns: during alleged burglaries, robberies, or even traffic violations, when police officers were anxious when approaching drivers or when they covered their colleagues. Sometimes, the officers drew their handguns before they had even brought their car to a halt at the scene of a reported crime, hoping to catch the criminal in the act. In most cases, however, we only found disillusioned victims or scared residents, for which officers had to draw one of two silver ballpoint pens from their dress-shirt pocket to write a report. Police officer Luz, who got into dangerous situations herself but had never used her firearm, said that "police officers look for opportunities to shoot. It is a way of showing their skills, to show that they been practicing on the range. They're told that rescuing a life is the best thing there is"—and that is especially the case when you must shoot or kill someone else.

One morning in May 2015, I received a call from Marcus. Someone had been shot close to the barbershop and the whole area was swarming with police—he thought it would be interesting for my research. After a short detour on my bike to avoid the police blockades, broadcasting vans, and yellow tape, I arrived at the barbershop, where both Fenix and Marcus were watching the news on a television screen. Directly in front of the shop was a police car with its lights on, guarding the perimeter. Watching the news on the television inside the barbershop, we learned that a middle-aged Black man had been shot close to the library in Culmer Park, one of Overtown's more popular parks. Marcus had heard the shots, which had been the outcome of a deadly encounter between a police officer, Antonio Torres, and Fritz Severe, a homeless man who frequently camped out in the park with his belongings. The interaction had escalated to the point where the police officer had used his gun and had shot and killed Severe, who had been holding an iron pipe in his hands. Rodolfo Llanes, the MPD chief of police, appeared on the news, and Fenix wondered what kind of excuse this "double-l dude" (a reference to the chief's name and indirectly the power inequalities between the Cuban and Black population in Miami) was going to come up with this time. Llanes told the journalists that the investigation was still ongoing, and that there was not much he could say at that time. Marcus and Fenix both blamed the police officer, turned off the news channel, increased the volume of the music, and returned to work.

In 2017, two years later, the Miami-Dade County state attorney's office had still not charged Torres with a crime, and he was still working as a Miami police officer. Five years later, in 2020, Miami city commissioners settled with Severe's parents and paid them $300,000 in compensation. The financial settlement, which came after a lengthy civil trial and in the absence of a criminal prosecution, speaks to the widespread impunity of police officers. In Overtown, residents speak ironically about "winning the ghetto lottery," referring to the amount of money a person can receive by prosecuting city officials and private companies who have violated their rights in one way or another.

Yet there are also other explanations and excuses for police shootings, which seem to normalize the structural nature of such violence. A couple of hours after the shooting of Severe, I spoke to one of Overtown's most known activists, whom the local media sometimes referred to as the "unofficial mayor" of the neighborhood. Indeed, as a community board member and long-term resident of Overtown, he was present at nearly all the local meetings that I attended. I wondered if he could tell me more about the shooting. Just as I had started saying, "There's just been a shooting at the ... ," he interrupted me:

> At the park. Yes. That happened because the regular [library] staff wasn't there. The regular staff would have never called the police: the man was not a dangerous person! But you got these people working the library system that get moved here and there. And they called: "Oh, he out there and he got an iron pipe. Get the police!" And the police killed him when they got there. I want to go to the library, and I want to know who was the one that set off the execution on the man. Because the chief said the caller pretended the man was so dangerous. Well to them, maybe so. But to the regular crew who live in the neighborhood, know all the people, [they]

know that he was not. Even the man [park manager, interviewed by the media] said the same thing. But you got some asshole in there that said: "Oh, this man is dangerous, this is the ghetto, this is Overtown, he gon' kill me, let me call the police and have them kill him!" All the children that go there know this man!

I asked the "mayor" what he thought of the role of the officer. He asserted forcefully that the homeless man's death was not to be blamed on the police:

> They need to arrest the person that made the call. Because that person lied and cost this man's life. The officer came with an attitude he would not have had if he did not get this bogus-ass information. So I don't hold anything against the officer.

According to the "mayor," the new staff members at the library were the ones responsible for the death of the man in the park, not the police officers, nor even the man himself, who had been wielding what could have been construed as a weapon. In his view, the library staff members should have known the implications of calling the police: namely, that if you call 911 and explain that you feel threatened, it is likely that a police officer will shoot.

What I found especially striking was the activist's immediate and explicit framing of the violent encounter in terms of a sense of responsibility and moral accountability that never contested the legality of gun violence. Instead of holding the police officer or even the victim himself responsible for the violence, the activist blamed an individual for the shooting who was not even legally involved in the physical encounter that took place. This illustrates how accountability may be interpreted once police gun violence is considered a given. Although other residents did frame the encounter as an example of police brutality, they were still primarily concerned with allocating individual liability and legal culpability: who had been at fault and might even be liable for prosecution? The police officer who shot a homeless man, the chief of police, the person who called the police, or the homeless man himself?

That gun violence is easily normalized, and to a certain extent even expected, is not limited to the realm of the police. In July 2019, Marshae Jones was indicted for manslaughter after she had been shot in the stomach by a co-worker, leading to the death of her unborn baby. Police officers in Alabama ruled that Jones had started the fight and had thereby endangered her baby's life. Although the charges against Jones were dropped once human-rights organizations became involved and publicly condemned the indictment, the case illustrates how the normalization of gun ownership and gun violence is mediated by a legal framing of victimhood. By initially indicting Jones, the authorities suggested that Jones should have known better than to antagonize her colleague, and that the possibility of gun violence should always be taken into account.

"What have we learned about 'gun violence,'" Patrick Blanchfield (2017) writes, "as a phenomenon and as a political cause, over the last five years?" Reflecting on the murder of Trayvon Martin and the mass shooting that killed twenty children and six adult teachers at Sandy Hook Elementary School in 2012 in Newtown, Connecticut, Blanchfield concludes that tragically enough, such events fail to provoke any substantial responses by themselves. To achieve more meaningful change, Blanchfield argues, requires a recognition of how guns are entrenched in American culture and politics—they are integral to the making of the American enterprise and are part of the reality of everyday life in the United States. This implies looking beyond particular interest groups (such as the NRA) and pieces of legislation (the Second Amendment), and acknowledging the interdependencies of state violence, both domestic and abroad, white supremacy, and the US military-industrial complex. Focusing on these "ugly social realities and broken institutions," Blanchfield points out, allows for a way to talk about the power that guns have enabled, and to think of alternatives.

In light of expected (police) gun violence, Dream Defenders offered a course on survival skills to local residents in 2020. They stated that it takes on average eleven minutes for an ambulance to get to a Black neighborhood such as Overtown; "So in other words, we all we got." The course is specifically aimed at people who carry guns legally or illegally, but mostly for those who feel that it is necessary to create a safe space for community members threatened by police gun violence and who want to learn how to manage a gun wound while waiting for professional medical assistance. The course illustrates what happens when systemic police brutality is an everyday threat for Black Americans, and how this translates into the responsibilization of individuals for their own safety.

Leaving the Gun Behind

In an unlikely turn of events, Olaf found the stolen Mini Cooper the next morning in an empty parking lot close to our home. It was completely unscathed, with only a trace of marijuana in the trunk. Olaf had removed the key the night it had been stolen, and while the engine of the Mini could run without a key, it could not start without one—meaning that once the thieves had stopped the car, there was no way to get it to run again. I drove behind my roommate in his BMW as he returned the Mini to our home.

Olaf was happy that he had found his girlfriend's car, but from that moment on he no longer wanted to live in the neighborhood. Although they had lived there without any trouble for several years, his mother said that she was not surprised to hear about what had happened the night the Mini had been stolen. Olaf made up his mind: he was going to leave the neighborhood and move back to the house his mother owned in Miami Beach. Olaf was Jewish, and he told me that he wanted to live among other Jewish people and neighbors who were more likely to feel involved should he become a victim of crime again. Fortunately, I was able move with him and could thus continue to be part of the everyday life of a main interlocutor during my research. In June 2015, just before we moved, I asked him a couple of questions.

> THIJS: Olaf, why do you want to leave?
> OLAF: I'm tired of fucking coming home and having to look and turn my head twenty times. Scared to get out of my car and having to lock myself behind the gate. I'm tired of having random people walking down the street worrying who they are, because they're looking to fucking break in and I am an easy target. I'm tired of all this shit, hearing this shit [referring to news about crime]. I just want to come home and not have to think about—just chill, get out my car, take my sweet time, leave my shit open when I have groceries. Simple things like that get fucking annoying. I want to take my trash out whenever I want and not worry what time it is.

THIJS: You're an easy target?

OLAF: There are people at night looking around for an easy target, and if you're not on point you get fucked. That's what happened to me the other night when I wasn't on point.

Olaf was tall, in his late twenties, and not particularly muscular or intimidating looking. Clearly informed by popular interpretations of victimization, Olaf reasoned that both he and his girlfriend were easy targets: he carried expensive musical equipment, and his girlfriend was fit and often came home in yoga pants, he explained. Interestingly enough, he also blamed himself for what had happened the night of the theft: he had not been "on point." In his experience, since he could not count on the police or the neighbors, it was his own responsibility to prevent and respond to crime. Unlike Alejandra, who felt much safer once her crime-watch group became popular in the neighborhood, Olaf felt his solution to insecurity was to move to Miami Beach.

The shotgun, however, did not travel with us to the new house (nor did his girlfriend, but that is a different story). After a trip to Spain for a couple of weeks, during which he gave me access to his room to use the shotgun to "scare off the Blacks," Olaf brought the weapon to the music studio where he worked, located farther west. In his view, the studio was located "in the ghetto," while our new house in Miami Beach was not.[3] Olaf's decision not to take the gun to Miami Beach was partly informed by his understandings of the kind of environment in which it would be necessary for him to use lethal force. Friends and family members had told him that living in the old neighborhood was unsafe, especially compared with Miami Beach. As dominant interpretations of crime and insecurity inform how and when guns are owned and used, it could be said that by not taking the gun to Miami Beach, Olaf was looking to escape specific assignments of responsibility, violence, and legal accountability.

Despite numerous and repeated attempts by activists and social movements, it is unlikely that gun laws will change in the foreseeable future. In the aftermath of the 2018 mass shooting at Marjory Stoneman Douglas High School in Parkland, Florida, protests emerged throughout the state, calling for more gun control. In Miami, students and residents joined the "Never Again" movement that survivors at the school started.

During various protests in the city, they called for stricter gun laws and a ban on the AR-15: the assault rifle the shooter had used to kill seventeen people. While minor changes to the law were made in Florida, include banning gun sales to anyone under the age of twenty-one, law makers and state officials, including Senator Marco Rubio, did not support any substantial changes.

Like state violence, private gun ownership laws reflect and sustain racialized interpretations of danger and insecurity, and often favor the shooter. In 2018, a white man and his family illegally parked their car in a disabled parking spot outside a Florida shopping mall. A local Black resident confronted them and pushed the white man, who fell to the ground. The white man then turned around and shot the Black man in the chest, killing him. The whole event was captured by the mall's security cameras. Local authorities, backed by the NRA, stated that they would not prosecute the killer because his actions were protected by the stand-your-ground law (Mazzei 2018). This and similar events have sparked local and national debates over private gun ownership, self-defense legislation, and racialized articulations of justice. Because guns in the United States are not only a powerful object embedded in popular culture but also central to claiming citizenship rights and intimately tied to the political economy, it is difficult for groups to protest private gun ownership or to advocate for tougher gun control.

Many US citizens have resorted to different ways of dealing with the injustices connected to police gun violence in everyday life. In Miami, Black residents as well as police officers increasingly use cell phones and body cameras to capture and replay policing encounters—as a way to mobilize support, to generate social media likes, and to make violent and racist policing more visible to others, or to use such photos and videos in courts of law to justify their actions. The widespread use of this visualizing technology with respect to police gun violence is the focus of the next chapter.

Figure 4.1. Mural in Wynwood, October 2016.

4

Looking through the Law

During a ride-along with Mark, a police officer with the MPD, he received a request from the police dispatcher. A 911 call had come in from a security guard who had just been punched by another man in a park in Downtown Miami. It was a code four call, meaning that Mark should use sirens and lights to arrive as quickly as possible. When we arrived on the scene, several officers already present were attempting to arrest a Black man, while numerous park visitors had gathered around the scene and were recording the struggle with their cell phones. The three officers were unable to get the man into a police car, and Mark used his baton to hit the man on his legs. Illuminated by the streetlight's glow, as well as the glare of flashing red and blue police lights, and surrounded by dozens of bystanders, the man began to shout, "Read me my Miranda rights!" He kept on repeating the sentence, louder and louder, before he finally succumbed to the officers' pressure and beating. The door of the police car slammed shut behind him. The car began to bounce, and you could hear the man shouting inside, trying to kick his way out. "He's gonna break it . . . ," one officer predicted. She was right. The tinted window came flying off and the man showed his head one more time, directing his speech at the audience and their cell phone cameras: "Read me my Miranda rights!"

The man that Mark and his colleagues were trying to arrest made sure to let the audience know that he felt the police officers were violating his rights. He demanded that they read him his Miranda rights aloud, suggesting the inconsistencies between police practices and legal rights. As every viewer of police procedurals knows, officers are supposed to read the standardized lines of legal rights and responsibilities to the person under arrest—but legally speaking, only before a verbal interrogation. In turn, the police officers seemed to consciously follow the exact textbook procedures for making the arrest and consulted with their superior officers regarding every increased use of force as the man refused to cooperate. Almost every one of the bystanders held a cell phone in their hand, silently following and capturing the scene through their digital screens. Not much later, police officers used leg cuffs to lock the man's legs behind his back and moved him into a different car. Mark came to stand next to me, wiping the sweat from his forehead. Looking at the numerous flashlights of cell phone cameras lighting up in the dark, he commented, shaking his head: "I'm here on the floor fighting for my safety, and their protection, and they're just standing over me with a phone, recording it. They only do that to use it against us."

Mark's skepticism comes at a time when cameras, especially cell phone cameras and police body cameras, have become crucial for addressing a wide range of citizenship-related issues, most notably police brutality. Mark explained to me that they had sought to proceed with the arrest "in a calm manner." In addition, they had made use of specific attributes, such as alarm lights, weapons, and uniforms, to rule out any perception that they were not in fact professional law enforcement officers and that their actions could not be justified to the growing crowd. "In order to uphold the illusion of law being omnipresent and effective," Thomas Blom Hansen notes, "law enforcement must appear as predictable, procedural, regulated, and above all, visible to the public" (2006: 282). While few policing actors who violate civil rights end up being prosecuted, let alone found guilty, Mark's understanding of the arrest suggests that cameras shape how police officers see and perform their professionalism and their own transgressions of law and procedure.

In turn, police officers have also relied on cell phone cameras and body cameras to record themselves or others while on duty, in part to protect and substantiate their personal and professional integrity. Politicians and presidents have endorsed the use of police body cameras, though for different and even opposing reasons. Some argue that body cameras protect civilians from police brutality, while others support the implementation of the technology to protect police officers from false accusations. Where victims of police brutality and others supportive of their claims see disproportional and unjustified violence, many officers and their supporters deny these allegations and claim self-defense or simply legal protocol. Indeed, there have been numerous instances in which perpetrators of police brutality, whose actions were recorded, were not convicted, leaving victims and their families with feelings of injustice, disillusionment, and emotional distress.

Vigilant citizens are expected to develop a heightened awareness of when and how their rights are violated, and they are expected to be capable of undertaking the necessary actions. Both police officers and citizens use cameras to capture their interactions, often to document visual evidence for personal or professional reasons. Analyzing how and when cameras are used in policing, I show how vigilant citizenship encourages people to *look through the law*, to see events, encounters, behaviors, and relationships in terms of legality and the (desired) functioning of the judicial system. Such a mode of looking reflects and reproduces a legal framing of everyday policing encounters. Here, I draw on the idea that many Americans feel legally entitled, that they expect the law to be on their side whenever they believe their rights are violated. Describing how ordinary people in the United States use the legal system, Sally Engle Merry (1990) discusses their legal entitlement based on a broad sense of rights. While many experience a loss of control in the face of different legal interpretations of perceived injustice, Merry shows how people continue to believe that the court can solve their personal problems. In doing so, she points to the cultural power of law that produces a sense of the world that, especially in the United States, is characterized by an individualization of blame and guilt.

"Legality," as Patricia Ewick and Susan S. Silbey also write, "operates through social life as persons and groups deliberately interpret and invoke law's language, authority, and procedures to organize their lives and manage their relationships" (1998: 20). Extending these analyses of legality to scholarship on visuality and policing, a legal way of seeing is grounded in the understanding that how policing is seen by others, most notably legal and political authorities, is informed by a way of looking and constructing differences: a gaze (e.g., Browne 2015; Mirzoeff 2011, 2016; Mulvey 1975; Urry and Larsen 2011). I specifically focus on the imagined relationship between visual evidence and judicial proceedings, and legal ways of differentiating right from wrong in everyday policing encounters.

The analytical application of looking through the law seems particularly useful in a world where residents, state agencies, and private companies increasingly litigate against one another at the intersections of human rights, constitutional, and criminal law (von Benda-Beckmann et al., 2009; Donovan, 2008). As John L. Comaroff and Jean Comaroff (2009) note, politicians and civil-society organizations increasingly imagine the law as a magical solution to social, political, and individual problems, reflecting a broader belief in the capacity of the law to establish and restore order. This tendency is evident in US politics, where politicians rely on litigation to have their claims supported and their policies accepted, or to refute accusations. Franz von Benda-Beckmann, Keebet von Benda-Beckmann, and Julia Eckert (2009) use the term "lawfare" to capture the shift of politics toward the legal courts, of democracy to law, and the transformation of political issues into technical-legal problems.

I found that police officers in particular tend to see and document their performances using visual "evidence" in order to protect themselves from legal prosecution and bureaucratic intricacies, and increasingly rely on cameras to do so. Cameras can hereby intensify existing notions of individual liability that are central to the concept of vigilant citizenship, allowing an "incident" of police brutality to be decontextualized from the larger racist and violent ideologies that inform policing practices and protocol. This modes of looking shifts our attention to the visual manifestations of objectification, the reification of gendered and racialized boundaries, and broadly shared forms of representation that often result in discriminatory and violent policing practices (e.g., Browne 2015). As government agencies, corporations, activist organizations, and individuals alike rely on the visual documentation of their practices as a form of legal insurance and a mode of showing transparency and professionalism, cameras have enabled imagined relationships between visual evidence and judicial proceedings to become rooted in everyday life and in markets, policies, and laws.

Recording the Police

Although police officer Mark felt uncomfortable being recording during his work, monitoring police activity is not necessarily new. Organized groups and networks such as CopWatch have existed in the United States since at least the 1960s, when the Black Panthers organized armed patrols that observed and documented police practices from a distance.

While government agencies sought to repress such organized efforts, "copwatch groups have risen up in recent years, spurred by controversies over police killings, and the spread of cell phone cameras among rich and poor" (Fan 2019: 65). Recent developments in consumer technology and legal precedent have enabled more people to capture police brutality and racial injustice in more detail, and to circulate these videos and images globally.

The ACLU, for example, has developed a cell phone application through which civilians can record police officers and directly upload this material to the organization's servers. During the Memorial Day weekend I discussed in chapter 1, I joined several ACLU volunteers who walked around as "legal observers," ready to capture violent police practices with their cell phones. The human-rights organization writes that legal observers can act as eyewitnesses and document "any incidents of police misconduct" or any violations of civil rights.[1] According to their website, these observers are trained to be "as objective as possible so that their documentation can be used as evidence if police misconduct or obstructions to constitutionally protected free speech are challenged in court." Despite this, the police did not seem to mind or feel threatened by these legal observers, and seemed comfortable in speaking of them and myself during the weekend.

In her work on photography, Susan Sontag (2003) explains that cameras have the unique characteristic of combining an "objective" record with a personal testimony. A personal testimony recorded by a mobile camera, in particular a cell phone camera, is easily seen as more authentic than a professionally shot image. Often shot by amateurs, these videos lack proper lighting, composition, and appear spontaneous, unstaged, and unmanipulated. They could therefore be interpreted by a larger audience not present at the scene itself to be an exact representation of "what really happened." Images have increasingly acquired a general authority over the imagination, superseding the printed and spoken word. In a way, Sontag explains, the photographic image has become hyperreal, more real than reality, blurring the difference between "a faithful copy or transcription of an actual moment of reality and an interpretation of that reality" (2003: 26). A significant body of scholarship in and beyond visual anthropology has sought to understand the role of photography in the production of "evidence" and its relationship to policing.

While the widespread availability of cameras has often been interpreted as a form of power leveling, as a way of escaping a state-centric gaze that delineates the difference between right and wrong, we know that seemingly incontrovertible visual evidence is by no means certain to result in pronouncements of legal culpability or convictions of wrongdoing. "There is something about how we fetishize these kinds of videos," John L. Jackson writes about recordings of police brutality, "that speaks to how naïve we all continue to be about the empirical self-evidentiality of visual 'proof'" (2015: 6). Indeed, the belief that cameras empower their users persists, whether or not this is supported by the desired judicial proceedings and political endorsement.

The frequent mismatch between apparent visual evidence and judicial outcomes is particularly evident in the context of policing. David Correia and Tyler Wall (2018) introduce the term *copspeak* to indicate the language through which the police are idealized as antidote to disorder, a discourse that continues to justify intrusive and harmful practices. Without addressing the capitalist and racialized nature of policing, and with the reality that police officers are fundamentally agents of violence in mind, Correia and Wall suggest that the recording of policing practices is unlikely to effect significant change. "Police worn cameras," as Lyndsey P. Beutin writes, "strengthen a system built on structural racism, rather than ameliorate its injustices" (2017: 5).

This is perhaps best illustrated by the case of Rodney King. In 1992, a video was made public capturing four Los Angeles police officers assaulting King, an African American man, with extraordinary force: fifty-six baton blows, seven kicks, and four Taser shots. Seventeen other police officers looked on. In the case against these officers, the prosecution viewed the video as the most objective piece of evidence imaginable, because it clearly showed the identified officers' wrongdoings. In fact, the prosecution was so convinced of the power of this visual evidence that they did not even call on Rodney King to testify but relied solely on the video as their primary witness during the trial. The lawyers who defended the police officers, on the other hand, urged the judge and jury to see the event through the officers' eyes, rather than through the camera's lens. They humanized and contextualized the officers involved, juxtaposing King's body language and position with those of the "anxious" and "threatened" officers. The assault was systematically categorized into distinct uses of force, each with a different level of severity and justification, which were then weighed against the LAPD's manual on beatings. As a result, and despite the visual recording of the beating, only one of the four officers was initially convicted of excessive use of force by the non-Black jury, which included NRA members and former military officers (see Butler 1993; Miller 1998).

In her analysis of the trial, Judith Butler argues that the video of the assault was seen within a "racially saturated field of visibility" (1993: 15). She suggests that jurors did not ignore the video but, rather, interpreted the "evidence" through a "racist interpretive framework to construe King as the *agent* of violence" (1993: 16; original emphasis). Within such a framework, Blackness is seen as the source of danger, and whiteness as in need of protection from this threat, making it difficult to see the violence of white supremacy and racial injustice. Through such a white gaze, King was seen as a threat, and the police officers were framed as the necessary defenders of a sovereign power.

The video visualized for many the reality of police violence and became a symbol of the disproportionate use of that violence against Black civilians—which is, furthermore, carried out with impunity. The case incited riots across the United States—an evident sign that many understood the King beating to be exemplary of structural conditions. Yet the case and its aftermath also demonstrate the workings of a legal way of watching, as collective experiences of injustice and police brutality increasingly became framed in an individualized fashion and legal terms. In public debate and the judicial proceedings that followed, the King beating was discussed as something extraordinary—as if violent and racist police practices were "intrusions upon ordinary situations" (Gooding-Williams 1993: 1). It is a frame that emphasizes the dramaturgical aspects and theatricality of the encounter, and which "constructs social events as transient curiosities that have accidently supervened on the circumstances of day-to-day life" (Gooding-Williams 1993: 1). While the King case fits within a longer tradition of white violence against Black people in the United States, from Jim Crow–era lynchings to the killing of George Floyd, governmental agencies still portrayed it as an exceptional incident, obscuring the structural conditions supporting such violent practices.

It is exactly this combination of an individualized reading of policing practices and the legal approach to culpability that this looking through law enables and reinforces. Citing Allen Feldman (1991: 109), Ruth Wilson Gilmore states that "arrest is the political art of individualizing disorder" (1993: 28). Despite the attempts of civil-society organizations to contest such readings, many people across the United States tend to see violent policing practices as incidents that can or should be solved through judicial proceedings. As a result, news reports and everyday discussions tend to examine the actions of individual police officers and victims in detail and through legality, still emphasizing the extraordinary character of such encounters in a way that makes it difficult to see them as an everyday (and often unrecorded) reality for many people.

Such a legal way of seeing policing practices and surveillance strategies reproduces and conceptualizes "blackness through stereotypes" as "the mere presence of blackness gets coded as criminal" (Browne 2015: 20). Looking at policing through a legal mode of looking perpetuates a juridical-oriented system of documentation. This makes it more difficult to address injustice in ways that go beyond culpability and result in actions other than (often unsuccessful) litigation.

In other words, through their use of cameras, state agencies are able to support individualized explanations of, and solutions to, police brutality.

Legal Potentiality

During my research, there were many occasions on which visualizing technologies were used in ways that speak to the imagined workings of the camera's legal potentiality. Before I was able to join the Miami Beach homeless outreach program, I had to do a drug test at the Mount Sinai Medical Center. After handing over the evidence—a document stating that I indeed had not used any illegal substances in the past few days—I joined a small team in a van in the middle of the night to search for people sleeping outside. Several police officers accompanied us, both for our protection but also to indicate that this was a government-led program that people should take seriously. Until dawn, staff members used a mobile tablet to record their interactions with anyone they found lying on benches, stairs, or on the beach. Taking pictures and short videos that they added to the profiles of people already in their database, the homeless outreach program offered various basic services such as shelters and drug treatment programs. Still, they had to document their encounters carefully. The tablet's camera allowed them to record the "evidence" that people had denied their services: proof that they had willingly broken the law and ignored requests to sleep elsewhere, which could be used to justify the involvement of law enforcement.

In the context of policing, however, cameras are particularly used to capture the actions of police officers. After driving against traffic on Ocean Drive with sirens and headlights blaring, and taking shortcuts through back alleys, MBPD police officer Alf and I arrived at the scene where three to four scooters were lying on the ground, and one man was already in handcuffs as an MBPD golf cart had arrived before us. An accident had turned into a fistfight, as I heard later. The man in handcuffs was shouting that he did not cause any harm, while officers put handcuffs on another. As I watched the scene, a security guard from a club next door asked me whether I was a witness and wanted to testify. "They want to help the police," Alf told me later. Many people walk away from such scenes, so the security guard had been trying to assist the police by gathering witnesses. After a while, both suspects were released from their handcuffs, as they apparently were not under arrest, after all. "If only we had cameras . . . ," the security guard remarked before going back to work.

Later during Alf's patrol, a call came in for backup for two police officers (one in training) who had stopped a car and were currently writing a ticket. We arrived at the scene, where we observed them at work. Because of the media attention that had followed the police killings of Michael Brown and Eric Garner, Alf told me, it was now required that a second officer should be present at any scene, as potential witness and "extra" officer in case something should happen. Alf explained that the officer who killed Garner had been alone; he believed that having a colleague present could have prevented the "incident." With blue and red alarm lights reflecting on his face, we talked about the accusations of racial profiling by the police and the mandatory body cameras coming sooner or later. "At the end of the day," Alf argued, "services delivered to the people here will decrease in quality. I will stop checking extra license plates. That is not my problem: I don't live here. I just bought a house in Broward. I'm not the one living here where people can go unchecked." Alf believed that public services would decrease in quality if he had to follow clear procedures that could be checked up on by any citizen who asked for a copy of the film once the report had been filed. His concerns also touched on the privacy of the officers: What if he needed to go to the bathroom? What about making fun of his supervisor?

Like Alf, some police officers feared that body cameras would affect how they go about their job: they told me that the presence of a body camera would prevent them from following their intuition. Officers often described police work as a "legal gray area" that required officers to approach "out-of-place-looking" individuals, sometimes without any clear reason other than intuition. The fact of wearing a body camera, however, might force them to have to prove probable cause, the reasonable grounds to believe that a particular person has committed a crime, or is about to violate the law, that affords police legal permission to stop and search people or their vehicles. Apparently unbeknownst to these officers, their complaints about the potential effects of body cameras on their policing behavior in fact supported proponents' reasoning. Officers themselves suggested that they would no longer be able rely on their "intuition" and would have to follow the letter of the law whenever they interacted with civilians, which was exactly what activists in Miami were seeking to achieve. Other policing actors, especially security guards, had similar perceptions. Sitting next to Santos at the bar in South Beach, his manager came to stand next to us and pointed to all the cell phones he saw in the hands of the customers. "With all these phones, I can no longer just throw people outside: someone will video it and sue us."

Policing scholars might find this exemplary of what they call "discretion": the unchecked power of police officers to enforce the law however they want. "By definition," Mark Neocleous writes, "the exercise of police discretion defines who is deviant in any social context and how that deviance is controlled" (2000: 99). Discretion, in other words, allows the police to enforce the law in a selective, and thus often racialized, fashion. More than legal codes and police cultures, policing as a form of state power is shaped by how police officers, as "street-level bureaucrats," exercise their right to use force. While Miami police officers understood their practices to be surrounded by legal uncertainties, Neocleous points out that this actually works as intended. Police officers therefore do not need much more than "reasonable suspicion" to legitimize their actions.

Although acting without probable cause always made a police officer susceptible to legal prosecution, the body camera caused many officers to frame their work in more explicitly judicial terms. Some officers, facing the looming "threat" of having to wear a body camera, even switched jobs and became instructors at the police academy, rather than having to engage in police work that involved encounters with the public. As one instructor explained to me, "It wasn't the time for officers like us to walk the streets." To him, that body cameras were deemed necessary, to check and control the actions of individual officers, meant that he could not work in the way he considered most effective. These police officers' initial responses suggested that body cameras could decenter the importance of "personal experience" (and its relation to racial profiling) within police work, in favor of more juridical interpretations.

However, I also encountered many police officers who saw potential benefits to wearing a body camera. During a short stop on the streets of Miami Beach, one officer walked around, slamming his hands on his large chest protected by body armor. "Bring 'em on," he said. "Everything will be on tape, so whenever I tell that motherfucker to take a seat, eight fucking times, and he doesn't do it, I have to force him down, what's he gonna do?" This was his emotional response to the number of complaints and internal investigations that he and many police officers in Miami were dealing with, a frustrating and time-consuming hassle, which many found stressful as it could potentially affect their future careers as law enforcement officers. Online searches using the names of the officers whom I met indicated that most of them had been involved in some kind of legal issue. Some had even been temporarily suspended or reassigned to an administrative task. Officers were thus often consciously aware of how the public perceived them and were actively concerned with preventing civilians from complaining to their superiors about their behavior. They believed that the body camera could lower the number of complaints, as the technology would prove that they had been adhering to the law and formal policies.

Here, Miami police officers focused on the legal potentiality of the cameras: they expected future recordings to mark police practices as either legal or illegal, but they also anticipated the cameras' potential to subject others to a similar gaze. Their interpretations and concerns reflect and define an imagined relationship between the camera's capacity to make something visible and the potential juridical consequences of this visibility—images continue to be understood as the ultimate evidence of whether an individual has acted lawfully or unlawfully. Officers also pointed out that "if people want police by the book, they're already arrested when they don't directly listen to an officer." While attending classes for police recruits, I observed one instructor warn his class that the media was not their friend: journalists were only out there to highlight police brutality and confrontational encounters, and showed little to no interest in other, more positive, sides of the work they did in society. This media attention encouraged members of the wider public to record police officers with their cell phones, he argued.

The legal potentiality of cameras, however, does not stem solely from their technological affordances. More broadly, it connects to what John Tagg refers to as the establishment of a "new regime of truth" (1988: 61), as government agencies and international companies have developed a proliferating documentation system that stresses the importance of collecting and saving evidence. As Corinna Kruse (2015) also explains, this system of producing (forensic) evidence through juridically oriented documentation—which has emerged and expanded across institutions, from hospitals and schools to prisons and police forces—relies on highly diverse and arbitrary knowledge practices, and on often conflicting technologies and legal and social practices. It also shapes how victims of violence understand their own suffering, as Sameena Mulla (2014) illustrates in her analysis of institutional imaginaries of evidence and practices of forensic intervention surrounding sexual violence. Forensic nurses tend to focus on collecting evidence, "blending the work of care and forensic investigation into a single intervention" (2014: 4). This "medico-legal" configuration shifts the emphasis from healing to juridical reckoning, instilling feelings of revictimization in victims of sexual assault, as most of the evidence collected never makes it to court.

As policing and photography evolve together, and recent innovations have made the technology more mobile and convenient, cameras have expanded and reinforced this juridically oriented system. As Stacy E. Wood (2017) points out, the rapid development of video documentation has allowed corporations to establish infrastructures that privatize the security and archiving of footage, while also challenging existing ethical and legal standards for the use of audiovisual material as evidence in court. She argues that partly because of the emergence of these unregulated infrastructures, it is unlikely that cameras, and police body cameras in particular, will be able to increase transparency and fix "complex and interlocking historical and socio-political realities" (2017: 41).

Yet the camera's legal potentiality is not only embedded in the wider media ecology of state-issued body cameras. Various governmental policies and corporate efforts have strengthened the perceived relationship between visual evidence and judicial proceedings in the broader use of visualizing technologies. In a twist of fate, decades after the Rodney King incident, the same company that fabricated the electric stun gun that the officers used against King (Taser, now a worldwide supplier of the technology) has begun to promote the usage of (body) cameras. Targeting police officers, an advertisement that I saw hanging in Miami's police stations conveyed the message that officers themselves are responsible for capturing the visual evidence necessary to protect themselves from any unwarranted judicial proceedings. The advertisement depicts a generic policing actor, either public or private, with a small camera attached to glasses sold by Taser. Underneath the image, the tagline read: "Testimony is interesting. Video is compelling." Here, Taser quite literally places the significance of an individual visual account above that of a verbal one for policing actors. And again in 2020, after the police killing of George Floyd and the ensuing protests, the company tweeted how their visualizing technology "helps eradicate racism and excessive force in the justice system." In a way, we might consider police cameras to be indicative of a broader belief that technologies are able to remove the "human bias" and improve accountability in policing.[2]

With or without visual testimonies of police misconduct, citizens have successfully sued police departments across the United States. The *Wall Street Journal* reported that the Miami-Dade County police department paid out roughly $2.7 million for misconduct claims between 2015 and 2020 (Calvert and Frosch 2020). In total, the twenty US cities and counties with the largest police departments have paid over $2 billion since 2015. Focusing on Chicago, the city with the highest number of fatal police shootings, Laurence Ralph (2020) highlights that payouts in the city have only increased in the past few years. And while cameras might offer victims of police brutality an increase in much-needed financial compensation, the technology, much like other forms of data-driven policing, does not actually improve police accountability by itself and might even reproduce the racialized workings of law and visuality.

The Photographic Performance

Directly after we left the MPD station and greeted the private security guard at the gate, MPD police officer Elrond got a call on his cell phone. His new lieutenant requested his presence at the entrance of Bayside Park in Downtown. There was no rush, so no need for him to turn on the alarm and sirens. After a short ride, we parked behind three other police cars, all with their blue and red lights flashing. Next to them was a large SUV attached to a tow truck, with a woman still sitting in the driver's seat, refusing to leave her car, which she had parked illegally. The police officers waited patiently, as requested by the lieutenant, the highest-ranking officer present. They gave the woman exactly half an hour to exit the vehicle by herself before they would intervene. The employees of the towing company were less comfortable and awaited the outcome of the negotiations by taking pictures of themselves on their cell phones while pointing their middle fingers to the cameras. After thirty minutes or so, and after all verbal attempts to get the woman out of her car had failed, the officers agreed that it was time to make an arrest.

The lieutenant instructed Elrond, a member of the SWAT team and the most muscular officer on scene, to handcuff the woman. The lieutenant seemed worried, however, and she ordered a sergeant to "stand by" with his cell phone to record the arrest. The woman sitting behind the wheel was Black, and I assumed that this heightened the lieutenant's anxiety and perhaps partly explained why she wanted the arrest recorded. Elrond reached inside the car and grabbed the forearms of the woman, who resisted verbally but obeyed physically. The sergeant recorded the whole interaction, and he only stopped recording when the backdoor of one of the police cars slammed shut behind the handcuffed woman. With the video saved to its memory card, the phone was returned to its holder attached to the sergeant's tactical belt, behind his gun. "It's the cherry on top of the cake," explained Elrond when we drove toward the City of Miami holding cells, located at the back of the MPD station. In case the woman filed a complaint against one of the officers, they could show the recording made by the sergeant that day. Filling out the report did not take Elrond much time, but during the rest of his shift he thought about why the woman had not left her car by herself. In his view, it was not worth getting arrested over.

Police officers with whom I spoke acknowledged that cameras allowed them to capture their perspectives whenever they felt it was necessary. In this case, however, the officers used a personal camera to record a video that the officers themselves could save in a place they could always access, unlike the expected body cameras, over which they would have much less control. The use of personal cameras has become increasingly popular among police officers, and the cell phone is an essential part of an officer's tactical belt, where it is locked in place alongside a handgun, Taser, flashlight, and ammunition.

Scholars have long emphasized that policing can be understood as a dramaturgical performance. As Peter K. Manning writes, "much of policing action is an attempt on the part of the police to dramatize their actions and to conceal or make less than salient their other more frequent but less impressive activities" (1978: 487). Manning argues that attempts to reform policing and address systemic violence have failed precisely because they were aimed at these performances, rather than the underlying premises and institutional aims. Drawing on this approach, Julia Hornberger (2011) analyzes police performances in terms of a "front" and "back" stage. She explains that these stages reflect different realms of policing: the "front stage" being the legalistic appearance, and the "backstage" the visible and tangible violence that overrides the law. Hornberger concludes that few officers are actually able to transform their performance into something congruent with the law, and as a result everyday policing continues to involve violent and extralegal practices.

With their legal potential to make things visible, cameras could plausibly compel people to act in accordance with the law. Yet it appears that people seem primarily concerned with how legal their actions look and might be viewed. I refer to this as the *photographic performance*: the ways in which people behave when they realize that a camera is switched on and capturing the scene. Cameras do not necessarily encourage officers to refrain from illegal and violent practices. In fact, they might even accentuate a legal reading of an otherwise blatantly unjust encounter, for instance, when a police officer is acquitted despite disturbing footage. By eliciting such photographic performances, I suggest, cameras emphasize the legal look of policing—its "front stage"—and in doing so overexpose individual behavior in a context of institutionalized violence.

As the visual documentation of policing practice increasingly supersedes written documentation, police officers seem to think and act differently about their own professionalism and transgressions of law and order. More specifically, they seem concerned with what Mirco Göpfert calls "bureaucratic aesthetics": a form of street-level bureaucracy that captures the intersections of official norms and informal practices, "between legal and pragmatic reasoning" (2013: 331). Göpfert shows that police officers construct accounts of their own practices through documentation, specifically the writing of daily paperwork, which involves manufacturing a report that is aesthetically satisfying to them. Similar to how Göpfert explains the way in which police officers write reports, police officers use cameras to document their own work, and in doing so, construct a perception of professional law enforcement where everyday police performances and legal reasonings increasingly become one and the same.

While recording may prompt police to perform their duties in a way that "looks legal," state agencies and affiliated organizations also expect civilians to follow a specific "script" during such encounters. Ideally, their performance should minimize (or even prevent) the risk of being a victim of police brutality. During meetings organized by activists in the Black police precinct in Overtown, a pamphlet created by the National Black Police Association (NBPA), an advocate forum for "minority police officers," was distributed. The pamphlet aimed to provide local residents with specific instructions on how to behave when stopped by a police officer. For instance, it advised them on what their performance should look like, to minimize the risk of escalation and violence. The document explained to Overtown's residents that if they acted in a particular way, they could avoid a confrontational outcome with law enforcement officers and the potential injury associated with such confrontations. Although it did explain that "every situation is different," it was distributed by national and local organizations as a way of suggesting that, as long as you followed certain microbehavioral guidelines based on the law, a police officer would not see you as a potential threat. This illustrates a more widespread understanding that the outcome of a policing encounter would largely depend on a recognizably law-abiding performance.

During an interview with local activists and supporters of the NBPA, one of them explained to me that young people need to learn how to deal with law enforcement—don't reach in that glove compartment! Wave your hands outside the car window, *ask* if you may reach for your papers in the compartment. I would love not to have my "problem" [being profiled due to being Black], but law enforcement has every right to know where you are going, and people should know this and deal with this.

She explained that she had recently been pulled over by a police officer herself, and her five-year-old daughter had thought that the police would shoot them. "But I kept my hands on the wheel. Young people, you know how every teenager is, are much more aggressive, they need to be informed how to behave during the encounter with police officers." This information also involves encouraging Overtown residents to shift their focus toward individualized solutions, focusing on how they should perform in a passive manner when dealing with a highly racialized law enforcement apparatus. Images captured by a camera can be used to uncover which individual was at fault, how, and when: *looking through the law*, questions of who did not stick to the script, and whose performance went awry, become of increasing relevance. Mobile camera technology affords a microanalysis of an incident, exposing the details of a person's behavior. In so doing, it reinforces a tendency to ascribe the violation of rights to a particular individual and their behavior.

Looking through law not only shapes performances, encouraging individuals to behave in a manner that looks lawful; it also filters out other, intimate, emotional interactions while privileging legal susceptibility. A short *New York Times* documentary called *The Rise of Body Cameras* (McDonald 2017) illustrates how police body cameras can influence emotional and interpersonal relationships and interactions. The documentary shows footage of a Chicago police officer shooting Paul O'Neal, an unarmed man, in 2016. We see in the depicted events directly after the shooting, the officer panics and turns to a colleague for comfort. The colleague does not want to talk to him, however, and points with her index finger to the body camera on her uniform. What she expresses with this gesture is a reminder that everything he says will be recorded, and can and will be used against him during police and legal investigations. The shooting was horrendous, and an unarmed man was shot and killed. The camera did not prevent this from happening. In addition, it deterred empathetic interaction, as the officer responsible was left alone in the immediate aftermath. Although at the time of writing body cameras are not yet standardized equipment for every police officer in the United States, this short documentary illustrates how the technology could soon affect interpersonal interactions and solidarity among police officers.

MPD police officer Luz expected that police body cameras would further exacerbate a set of individualized beliefs and practices within the MPD. She specifically mentioned the term "CYA" (short for "cover your ass"), referring to the many ways that police instructors teach recruits how to deal with other officers who clearly violate civil rights in their presence, for example, by using excessive force against an arrestee. "Whenever you see another officer doing something bad," MPD instructors told their recruits on a walking tour through Overtown, "back off." Luz explained how this attitude of CYA informs the way police officers document their involvement in various cases and their interactions with local residents and fellow officers, making sure that their actions can always be seen in accordance with legal guidelines and police protocol, and thus minimizing the risk of legal prosecution.

While this chapter is primarily concerned with the workings of a legal mode of looking in policing, especially in terms of how police officers see and perform their own practices in everyday encounters, it is important to recognize the different epistemologies at play in the use of cameras. Indeed, cameras have allowed the BLM movement and organizations supportive of the cause, both past and present, to mobilize against white supremacy and institutionalized racism. Recordings of police brutality and social media platforms have made possible what Yarimar Bonilla and Jonathan Rosa (2015) call a "political temporality" in which people have formed around collective grievances and opposed police practices. Although a gaze often reifies stigmatized representations and reproduces historical inequalities, people also oppose such forms of visualization: they construct counterhegemonic visual cultures and configurations to negotiate and oppose existing depictions of themselves and others (see e.g., Gillespie 2006). Cameras, too, enable a way of looking otherwise.

Looking Otherwise

Marcus and Fenix carefully wielded their electric razors, creating precise, customized haircuts to the sound of Future's latest rap album playing through the barbershop's loudspeakers. The air was filled with the scent of hairspray and alcoholic disinfectant, misted liberally over the customers' heads after each cut. Although both hairdressers were highly skilled and efficient, the line of visitors seemed a little overwhelming for them that afternoon in July 2015. Fenix took short breaks, smoking a cigarette outside and checking his phone before rushing back in. This was definitely not a good time to disturb either of them, so I was happy to be able to chat with those waiting on the chairs next to me. Marcus's father entered, and as Marcus unplugged the audio cable from his cell phone, the buzzing sound of Fenix's razor suddenly became audible. I had seen his father before, but we had never had a chance to talk. When I told Marcus's father about my research in the neighborhood, he mentioned several negative experiences he had had with police officers. Some had occurred recently, some several years ago, and many of these encounters had taken place in Overtown. Other customers gathered around us and began to share their experiences and frustrations with Miami's police departments, accusing them of institutionalized racist practices. The customer who was getting his hair cut tried nodding carefully to show his agreement, even as Fenix pushed his head forward for the cut.

To show me what they were talking about, one of the customers picked up a video camera and played several recordings of interactions between neighborhood residents and police officers. I saw videos of MPD officers arresting individuals near the barbershop and of black undercover cars parked across the street. During a previous visit, Marcus told me that he knew they were police cars, because most vehicles owned by public officials have a license plate that ends with the letter x. Besides, the windows of these cars were so darkly tinted that it would have been illegal for a civilian to have had them installed. Most of the videos had been shot from the angle of the barbershop's front door, where Marcus could position himself. The door could only be opened from the inside, so he could lock himself in should the situation escalate.

On my next visit to the Overtown barbershop, I found Marcus alone playing *Grand Theft Auto* on his PlayStation. I learned that Marcus kept the camera close by, on a shelf below a mirror decorated with drawings by his son and pictures of family and friends. Marcus used the camera to shoot music videos and marketing material for his shop, but he had also bought and used it specifically to record police officers in the neighborhood. Indeed, he switched it on whenever he expected to interact with them. The camera was Marcus's way of responding to what he called the "corruptification" of local police departments, by which he meant both the numerous violent practices perpetrated by officers and their conscious attempts to conceal them. "The police are the biggest gang out there," he told me, indicating the lengths to which they will go to cover up their illegal activities internally. Since the MPD would never critically address its racist and violent policies by itself, Marcus reasoned, recording the actions of individual officers was the only way of making police brutality visible, of giving it some kind of meaning beyond and outside a single encounter.

In Marcus's view, it was not a matter of if but when officers would physically or verbally assault him. He figured that this was most likely to happen during his bike ride home. To deal with this sense of insecurity, Marcus regularly hung his camera around his neck, where it dangled in front of his chest and recorded his commute from home to work and back again. For Marcus, that police officers wore body cameras did not mean much in terms of ensuring his personal safety, or that of other residents of Overtown for that matter. "For people to be safe, everyone needs to wear a body camera," Marcus argued. He was particularly suspicious of certain police officers whom he knew by name—he did not expect them to change their behavior. Indeed, he experienced an increase in police hostility whenever he switched on his camera. Marcus was interested in the idea that he could use these recordings in future court cases. At the time, as we saw earlier, he was being charged with resisting arrest and had asked his attorney to look for any footage from nearby security cameras to prove otherwise. Marcus thus primarily recorded the police to share these videos with others, both on social media platforms and with customers and friends in the barbershop.

Looking past these legalizing and individualizing effects, Marcus saw more structural and deeply rooted inequalities through his camera lens, reflecting differentiations of citizenship along the lines of race, class, and residential location. In their analysis of the antistate-violence protests in Baltimore in 2015, Kalfani Ture and Anthony Angelo Gualteri (2017: 6) also write that "an ongoing strategy for these mobilizations relies on cell phone technology to increase awareness of Black and Brown deaths at the hands of police." This is also what Allissa V. Richardson (2020a) calls "Black witnessing," a way of looking back at authorities in times of crisis or protest. Through the use of cameras, Black witnessing "forges a historic narrative that links new atrocities against African Americans, such as police brutality, with the original corporeal sins against Black people: slavery and lynching" (Richardson 2020a).

This use of cameras shows that visualizing technologies, according to Ariella Azoulay, can also be a useful space in which to escape a sovereign power, to "reformulate the boundaries of citizenship" (2008: 24). Because photography and videography allow for multiple meanings, she explains, they allow for an experience and enactment of rights and responsibilities aside from the exclusive relationship between a citizen and a nation-state. This involves a citizenship that is not subject to the authority of state agencies, because the latter cannot completely control the way in which a particular image is interpreted. Azoulay suggests that cameras are an excellent tool for pursuing alternative political agendas and resisting contemporary power relations. Not because they give people control over how videos and images are interpreted by others, but because the technique to make visible has altered a way of seeing, a way of escaping a state-centric view of what citizenship should look like in everyday life. Azoulay concludes that everyone involved in photography is automatically a contributing member of a political community, a citizen of photography of sorts.

The use of cameras as an objective eyewitness account is, however, still very much connected to the workings of the US legal system and how local residents experience and understand the workings of the law (Fuller 1994; Pirie 2013; Rosen 2006; Sarat 1990). This makes it a significant challenge to look otherwise in the context of everyday policing. Many residents perceive and use laws as their go-to instrument to address a broad range of individual experiences of wrongdoing and feelings of inequality; these perceptions and practices are strengthened by the strong and active presence of legal professionals (*abogados*) in daily life throughout the city. While quantitative findings contest the assumption that the United States is a litigious society—apparently only a surprisingly small minority of people actually file lawsuits and claims—people still feel legally entitled (Engel 2016; Merry 2012).

This legal consciousness is not necessarily differentiated by subject position or degree of intoxication: disenfranchised residents also hold dear the beliefs that the courts will offer some form of justice to them and that systemic violence is the outcome of individual misconduct. Many policed civilians I spoke with in Miami demonstrated both a deeply felt cynicism vis-à-vis the law and a strong desire to be proved wrong—they persisted in hoping that society functioned according to the rule of law. Ruth was partly right: "Apparently white people need to see us lying dead in our own blood before they believe us." As the Taser advertisement points out, verbal accounts of racialized police violence are, unfortunately, less persuasive. While skeptical about their chances of winning an individual court case, these citizens still idealized the rule of law, hoping that justice would also be available for them.

Visualizing technologies alone are insufficient to escape the workings of a legal mode of looking. Obviously, something more than "compelling" videos is needed to change the way such violations of civil rights are seen and understood. But cameras do enable the creation of ways of seeing cultural and political change that do not privilege an individualized and legal reading of police work. Dream Defenders, the Miami branch of Black Lives Matter, connected various distinct, albeit related, issues, including the minimum wage, the occupation of Palestine, racial segregation, and sexism. Through protests, workshops, classes, and other forms of civil disobedience, they aimed to develop a broader narrative that allowed Black residents to politicize the violation of rights by defending nonwhite life, as one of the founders told me. More recent protests, both in Miami and elsewhere, show that camera recordings have brought together a wide range of people to challenge anti-Blackness in various institutions (see also Auston 2017). Indeed, cameras also enable a close reading of policing encounters, and the recorded videos can be used to share common feelings of victimhood and to experience moments of collective belonging. Yet we should be cautious when depending on visualizing technologies to expose inequality, and we should take into account how police officers themselves have incorporated the technology to produce visualities of professional law enforcement.

Like *copspeak* and its linguistic power, this legal mode of looking helps us to understand how police officers document their own practices and legitimize the use of violence through visualizations of legality. Making policing encounters visible through camera recordings highlights personal errors, allowing people to envision judicial proceedings and opportunities to sue individuals for their wrongdoing. This is also what Kamari Maxine Clarke calls the fictions of justice: "the reassignment of criminal responsibility to the individual and the myth of legal pluralism as a viable way to address violence through both international and national mechanisms" (2009: 4). While the production of these fictions warrants critical scholarship, we should also be concerned with how cameras are used to apply imagined workings of the judicial system in visualizations of everyday policing encounters. In particular, we should look at how law enforcement agencies document legal-looking performances that reflect and sustain a state-mediated gaze through which racialized and violent policing practices are legitimized.

The overabundance of images and videos of police brutality might normalize the experience of seeing such violence against Black bodies, giving it a certain ordinariness that perhaps even desensitizes people. This is perhaps an unintended implication of making such violence visible to a larger audience. Yet the violence recorded by cameras can also be seen as exceptional to a perception of policing as peaceful and transparent. As I have suggested here, this outcome of making racialized and violent policing visible is not simply a byproduct of the use of visualizing technologies. As developments in photography have informed policing practices since the twentieth century, police officers and governmental agencies have been quick to implement mobile cameras to their advantage—to capture and share their perspectives in their everyday work. Perspectives that, in their view, shows that they were under direct threat, responded in self-defense, and that they simply followed protocol. It therefore remains important to support visualizations of policing with a more macroperspective of anti-Black violence: to contest the limitations of the restrictive interpretative framework through which such racialized violence is seen and made sense of, and to look beyond explanations that zoom in on individual behavior, legal procedures, and criminalized bodies. In escaping such a way of seeing, LaCharles Ward (2018) recommends taking into account the potential of Black visual culture. Analyzing the work of visual and performance artists, Ward shows how these ways of looking provide a different understanding of Black life and death, which produces an imaginative space that is not "tethered to the logics of the state" (2018: 101).

Recording policing, either through body cameras or cell phone cameras, can be considered an act of vigilant citizenship. Police officers look to defend their professional integrity, to capture a perspective that they believe can also protect them from legal culpability and prosecution, because it shows that they did indeed do the right and lawful thing. Aware of the potential effects of videos and photos, this chapter has shown that police officers use the technology both to document their practices and to change their performances. This change, however, does not mean that they become any less violent, but rather that they perform policing and administer force in a way that looks more "legal." Yet recording policing actors through cell phones is also an act of citizenship—albeit one not in line with the vigilant ideal. This form of "Black witnessing," as Alissa V. Richardson also writes, "is not a denouncement of one's patriotism; it is an exercise of it" (Richardson 2020a). Although it is undeniably painful to record violence, by pressing record on their phones, people are "challenging a nation not to look away." Important, however, is not to look at these deaths casually; they should be "viewed like lynching photographs—with solemn reserve and careful circulation" (Richardson 2020b). Taken together, visualizing technologies and the politics of making visible enable a way of looking otherwise that is distinct from a legal mode of looking and a white lens of legality and visuality. This seems particularly relevant as police departments all over the world invest more money in visualizing technologies and media ecology to justify their practices and behaviors.

Like other groups organized around similar values and goals, Miami's Dream Defenders' efforts could appear a bit haphazard given the broad range of topics and issues that they covered. However, through efforts that centered around cultural and political changes, while incorporating other aspects of daily life, Dream Defenders and affiliated organizations looked for ways to establish feelings of solidarity and political community in terms other than those of criminal and civil law. Considering the significance of the law in everyday life, this is not an insignificant challenge.

Conclusion

American Values?

Launched in 2017, the cell phone application *Citizen* is a crime-tracking program that relies on public-safety data to generate real-time updates and notify its users of threats and crime in close geographical proximity. Marketed as a much-needed solution for residents living in "crime-ridden" urban environments, *Citizen* provides users with information believed necessary to navigate the dangers of everyday life. In a short promotional video showcasing the potential of the application, we see a *Citizen* employee monitoring 911 distress calls. She answers an emergency call concerning a "man with gun," a message that she then transmits to users of the application, warning those nearby. A mother with a young child in a stroller is alerted by the notification and decides

Figure c.1. "Trump does not represent American values," October 2016.

to walk into the opposite direction—away from "the man with gun"—and thus avoids potential harm. The video concludes by showing the New York City skyline at dusk, the city where it was first launched, while a graphic visualization of the *Citizen* network illustrates how its users are notified of a variety of threats in their respective areas. Threats that either require them to be cautious, as in the case of the "violent woman with hammer," or to be on the lookout for suspects, as in the case of the "cell phone stolen."

This suggested use of *Citizen* speaks to a broader assumption that more crime-related information empowers people, enabling them to make safer decisions. Not only do notifications inform users of the precise location of close threats and crimes, the app also encourages them to be more aware, to be on the lookout for any potential perpetrators and suspicious activity. The idealized outcome, as the video also shows, is that harm is prevented, crime is reduced, and criminals are caught in the act. *Citizen*, in other words, encourages people to be *vigilant*—to be aware, watchful, and willing to act when confronted with feelings of insecurity. In other promotional videos produced by *Citizen*, police officers always appear to be too far away to respond to a distress call in time. Even as they speed toward the scene with their flashing red and blue alarm lights, a video suggests that citizens are always closer and able to intervene more quickly. In these promotional materials, the police officer represents a willing and caring, yet incapable, state that is unable to provide the necessary protection for everyone in a timely fashion. Citizens, it's implied, should take on the necessary responsibility and take care of their own safety.

I only learned about *Citizen* after I had completed most of the writing for this book. Currently, it features a live-broadcast section, where users can share their support and prayers for those currently affected by crime through text and emoji. *Citizen* now has over ten million users and offers additional services through paid subscription services such as *Citizen Protect*. This latter service gives users access to a *Citizen* agent, who can be contacted when users want to call someone in order to feel safe. When connected, these agents can monitor the client's phone through the device's camera, motion sensors, and microphone, and alert authorities should they receive sounds or images of immediate distress. By no means a substitute for an actual emergency call, *Citizen* agents can only help navigate subscribers to safety: they still have to call 911 themselves to help these users.

Before it was called *Citizen*, the application had a different name: *Vigilante*. After Apple removed it from its online stores on the grounds that the term *Vigilante* carried a controversial connotation (to say the least), the developers decided to change the name. For them, this was a purely practical solution—it allowed them to regain access to users of Apple products—and it did not change anything about the intended workings of the application itself. It was as if the two terms could be used interchangeably, as if they meant the same thing in practice. Both the workings of the application and its name change from *Vigilante* to *Citizen* are illustrative of my analysis of policing in this book. Currently available in more than twenty cities across the United States, including Miami, *Citizen* is exemplary of current developments in urban safety. Widespread commercialized imaginaries of crime, anxiety, and fear, tied directly to idealized typologies of vigilant citizens–vigilant citizenship, continue to be a central premise in everyday articulations and experiences of policing.

Policing has always involved creating differentiated experiences of what safety and security mean in practice. This book examines how such inequalities are intensified both in and beyond encounters with police officers, and both within and beyond the institutional boundaries of their agencies. In a context of urban segregation and insecurity, the concept of vigilant citizenship shows how state power extends to the realm of civil society, where racialized and violent ideologies manifest in mundane aspects of daily life. Vigilant citizenship emphasizes that policing—as a structural and systemic form of violence—requires citizens be watchful, suspicious, and fearful of others. Vigilant citizenship cultivates and reifies existing distrust and racialized fears; yet it also individualizes these sociological phenomena. Throughout this book, I point out the insecurities that many residents experience, including police officers who look for ways to protect their professional integrity and physical safety. Of course, this is not to say that their vulnerability is not mitigated by the support they receive from police unions, politicians, and civil-society organizations. Rather, it is to point out how widespread feelings of insecurity are, and that police officers, too, experience the need to deal with these feelings as individual citizens.

From the opening story in which MBPD police officer Hernandez showed me his three knives, this book is concerned with how people understand what policing means for them and how this translates to daily practices. I seek to trouble traditional divisions between public and private policing actors, emphasizing the similarities in their experiences of safety and insecurity. I show that, precisely through its broader emphasis on individual rights and responsibilities, vigilant citizenship makes it harder for both policed citizens and policing actors to appreciate the systematic nature of racialized policing practices. This leads to a general misrecognition of the role of the state institutions and market forces that have created and legitimized the structural conditions of inequality and white control.

In chapter 1, we trace the interconnections between policing and socio-spatial inequality in Miami. Drawing on the experiences of Luz, Marcus, Fenix, and Santos, we explore broader experiences of inequality and violence, and examine how they navigate the urban landscape of a city that consists of pockets of safety, gated communities, and "ghettos"—and, above all, an urban environment characterized by high levels of exclusion and spatial and racial segregation. In chapters 2, 3, and 4, I discuss lateral surveillance, gun ownership, and cameras as three entry points for thinking through how vigilant citizenship mediates everyday policing. Marcus and Fenix were concerned with aggressive police officers in the vicinity of the barbershop, my roommate Olaf was afraid of violent intruders and burglars, Ruth had a complicated relationship with her drug-dealing neighbor, Luz was uncertain about her future and worried about how others perceived her qualifications as an officer, and Santos was frustrated with and fearful of the customers at his workplace. Most, if not all, of the respondents included in this book were affected by lateral surveillance, and relied on guns and cameras in their attempts to protect themselves, their loved ones, and their belongings.

In chapter 1, I draw heavily on the experiences of both Luz and Santos. To follow up on them, Luz eventually left the MPD after a series of distressing events and court cases in 2016. In early 2018, she contacted me with good news: she had been hired by the City of Miami—not as a police officer but as an analyst in the accounting department. Luz told me that she still missed her police work from time to time but was extremely happy that she had found a new position with all the same benefits. "It did turn out in my favor," she wrote me, supported by a picture of her behind her new desk. The last time we spoke she was living together with her boyfriend in North Miami. Santos left the bar at South Beach shortly after I left Miami for a pause in my fieldwork in October 2015. He had been offered a better position as a security guard at the contested construction of the Dakota Access Pipeline, where he worked for a couple of months. Afterward, when he returned to his hometown, he found work elsewhere.

In chapter 2, we trace how longstanding ideals of public vigilance have informed modern lateral surveillance practices in which citizens are encouraged, expected, and authorized to surveil one another. Examining these programs and activities, this chapter aims to show how state agencies shape political subject formation at a local level. Based on my experience with several lateral surveillance programs and practices, I found that they are likely to cultivate distrust, fear, and alienation, feeding into existing racialized and violent reactions by police officers and neighborhood-watch groups. State agencies, like the app *Citizen*, ask local residents to become part of a community of vigilant citizens in order to improve conditions of public safety. Yet this is a community whose members contextualize situations and actions through racial categories that generate forms of privilege and disadvantage.

Struggling with feelings of suspicion and distrust in her neighborhood, Ruth managed to find a beautiful, affordable, and brand-new apartment on the outskirts of Overtown. It even had a spare room for her son to come over and stay. To be honest, I was actually surprised that she had been able to find the necessary legal assistance to get herself out of her burned-out previous home. Before I left, I helped her to buy furniture for the new apartment and joined her on her balcony. She smoked a cigarette and wondered: "Maybe this whole gentrification is a good thing." She had felt hopeless in her old apartment, where the authorities seemed unable or unwilling to address the illegal practices of her neighbor. Perhaps, Ruth reasoned, gentrification might be the only option to ultimately improve living conditions for many residents like herself.

In chapter 3, we see how Olaf and others relied on guns for individual protection. Focusing on the legal framework of private gun ownership, we examine how self-defense becomes meaningful in everyday policing. Through the analogy of dogs, wolves, sheep, and sheepdogs, we consider private gun ownership as an extension of state violence and connect the possession of guns to clear displays of white vigilantism during periods of civil unrest. Guns are given a different meaning and status depending on whose hands they are in: some guns are perceived as contributing to public safety, while others are seen as threatening it. I explain how the ideal of vigilant citizenship materializes around gun ownership and use, how this informs differentiated experiences and enactments of citizenship, and how people navigate legal liability and reflect upon the ethics of using a lethal weapon against other human beings.

Olaf broke up with several girlfriends after the one who owned the Mini Cooper. He also moved again, from Miami Beach back to the old neighborhood, to a house close to the first place we shared. We have kept in touch, and he tells me that Miami is best enjoyed single. He leads several nonprofit projects that make it possible for primary school children to learn an instrument and play in a band. Once surprised by my research interest in Overtown, he became in turn surprised that the neighborhood "was not that ghetto after all." "Well," he added, "not the whole neighborhood at least."

In chapter 4, we examine how police officers understand and make use of cameras. Focusing on body cameras and cell phone cameras, we analyzed how the police document their own practices through notions of law and order. Concerned with legal-looking performances, police officers align themselves with attempts to tackle systematic police brutality as a problem of individual misconduct and legal oversight, rather than with attempts to address the underlying premises of a racialized order and state oppression. At the same time, I discussed how Black residents and activists can look past the camera's legalizing and individualizing effects. By situating the use of cameras within the broader BLM movement, I suggest that an increase in awareness of police brutality, in combination with a historical narrative of apartheid, can enable an alternative way of looking. Fenix left Marcus's barbershop in 2016. I had never heard about any quarrels between the two, but what I heard from Fenix is that he did not like the atmosphere at the shop and felt alienated because of his sexual orientation. He went back to working from his home in Overtown and advertised himself as a barber on social media. Marcus hired a new employee and went back to school to get a college degree.

While the police remain a central actor in policing—both in this book and in everyday urban life—these chapters situate police work in a broader context of security privatization, real estate development, housing policies, laws, and governmental programs. While police brutality continues to be central to the lived realities of urban and racial inequality, we have seen how such violence is more than a problem of the police. By mobilizing citizens, as well as emphasizing self-defense and vigilantism, state and legal institutions create inequalities in ways that extend beyond the actions of police departments. These are inequalities that are grounded in historical processes of apartheid, sustained by contemporary forms of white supremacy, and intensified by an ongoing expansion of state control in and over everyday life.

This book has shown how vigilant citizenship reproduces a social order based on the discrimination of Black Miamians; yet this book is not about convincing you, the reader, that policing reflects and sustains racism. Such an attempt to "uncover" the reality about policing would involve a logic similar to the use of police body cameras: that our primary concern should be looking for some kind of evidence that violent and racist policing is omnipresent. Making his way through extremely disturbing cases of police torture in Chicago, Laurence Ralph (2020) explains that his aim is not to reveal the realities of police brutality. "It would be insulting," Ralph (2020: 187) concludes, to suggest that scholars today could uncover something about policing that many (Black) Americans do not already know. While it might be tempting to examine policing as some kind of black box, waiting for the experienced researcher to find the ultimate evidence within, there remains little new to tell people who deal daily with systemic violence and structural conditions of inequality. What Ralph emphasizes is that policing is *intentional*: it is by no means an accident that we have to explain but, rather, the outcome of deliberate policies and laws that purposefully create differences, inequalities, and injustices. A long-term investment of public funding in fear—in police departments, state surveillance, and incarceration (at around $80 billion per year)—"maintains the racial caste system in the United States" (2020: 3).

This intentional inequality also works across institutions, actors, and settings. Whether or not police officers explicitly and purposefully mobilize racialized understandings of crime and danger, the heritage of the police as an institution makes it difficult for police officers not to reproduce the racial caste system in the United States. Yet this is not only a problem of the police, or of nonstate policing actors for that matter: it is also a problem of a broader belief in self-protection and related practices of self-defense. On a basic level, this means that getting rid of a racist police force still leaves us with those who act like vigilant citizens, such as George Zimmerman. On a deeper level, this means that the racial disparities seen in policing today not only stem from the state institution itself but also extend and materialize in various ways in social relationships and everyday interactions—indeed, they manifest in what it means to be a *citizen* in an American city. Regardless of one's professional status, vigilant citizenship prescribes that "good citizens" are fearful of Black Americans and act upon these feelings of insecurity. While defunding or abolishing the police seems like a necessary move to realize a more inclusive form of public safety, this book urges us to think through the policies that shape our citizenship as well.

Throughout my research, I found that vigilant citizenship also takes on an intimate dimension. It does not just exist within the public sphere, but also affects personal lives. Refuting Ken Plummer's polemic argument that citizenship tends to refer "to the social, civic, public world, not to individual, intimate, or private worlds" (2003: 15), I show how policing increasingly politicizes personal experiences and relationships. Lateral surveillance, for instance, reads everyday livelihood practices through narratives of safety and security. These are narratives that speak to idealized communities in a way that foregrounds the rights and responsibilities of US citizens in the context of policing. Guns are also highly personal. The numerous types and models available allow people to develop a personalized choice regarding their individual firearm. Alex, the manager of the Wynwood gun store, described his customers' different preferences to me: he sold pink handguns, very small weapons, and large assault rifles with a chainsaw attached to the barrel. Guns were also stored in the most intimate of places. Olaf was most comfortable with his shotgun under his bed, the same bed he slept in together with his girlfriend. Ruth hid her revolver in the back of her underwear drawer, or sometimes underneath her pillow. Many others indicated that they preferred to place their weapon on the nightstand next to their bed. In popular culture, guns are often loved and imagined as the best, if not the only, way for individuals to keep themselves safe. Perhaps this also helps explain the strong affection people display toward them in everyday life. Finally, cameras exemplify the intimate experience of policing in yet another way. Cell phones and personal cameras, generally bought and used to capture special and personal moments, are utilized in encounters with law enforcement. Videos of police officers, security guards, and aggressive residents are stored on devices that do not differentiate between public and private events. People interchangeably use social media and security apps, including *Citizen*, to record all kinds of interactions and relationships. Such examples show how the intimate experience of policing has increasingly become part of lived realities, at least in Miami.

I have used Miami as a case to discuss national trends and developments, to say something about the United States as a whole. During most of my fieldwork, I remained convinced that the city was not as politically active and involved as perhaps some other places in the United States. I read, for example, the work of Jan Nijman (2011), who argues that Miami is not a cohesive community and that transience is the city's defining characteristic. Nijman finds evidence of this exceptional transience in everyday life, where sports teams have difficulties building a loyal fan base, and political rallies and protests do not gather much support. In 2015, the walls of Marcus's barbershop were painted in the colors of Miami Heat, the local basketball team, and displayed some of its most renowned players. But a little under a year later, Marcus had completely redecorated the shop, explaining that the Heat theme had just been to attract customers when they were playing well. In 2006, massive immigration rallies were organized throughout the United States, protesting the restrictive reforms to immigration laws and policies. In Miami, the city with the highest proportion of immigrants in the entire country, the largest rally had only four thousand people, compared with five hundred thousand in Los Angeles. Illustrating this transience and individualization in a dramatic fashion, Nijman describes how Miami's more affluent residents move about the city: from their air-conditioned homes, in their air-conditioned cars, to air-conditioned offices and malls.

Miami seemed not as politically noisy and contentious as many other US cities as well. In November 2016, I was in Miami as Donald J. Trump was elected president for the coming four years. After attending a public viewing party, where several of those present had voted for Trump, Alfredo—my good friend and fellow graduate student—and I decided to continue watching at his home. We said our goodbyes with a shot of vodka: the night—or the morning after—was not going to get any worse for us anyway. Earlier that day, I had traveled to different voting stations and talked to several of my key interlocutors in Wynwood and Overtown. Marcus and my roommate Olaf told me that they had voted for Trump and were happy with the outcome. Olaf even went out in Wynwood to celebrate. In 2016, the "swing state" of Florida became a "red state," though most Miamians had voted for Hillary Clinton. Unlike other metropoles in the United States, however, there were no protests against the outcome of the election in Miami: a highly unequal city, where many residents identify as Latinx or Haitian American, but where nobody seemed willing to rally against Trump. I could not help but think of Miami's reputation as an apolitical city, where demonstrations and protests are surprisingly non-existent or small compared with other cities with large migrant population groups and such an unequal distribution of wealth.

But these representations of Miami—which I perhaps assumed a bit uncritically—changed only a few days later. Olaf called me, saying that he could not meet that night. Apparently, the I-95 ramp to Downtown Miami had been blocked by protesters. As many had done before, the protesters used the city's infrastructure as a stage for expressing their dissatisfaction and enacting civil disobedience. Still on the phone with Olaf and watching the news, I picked up my camera and ordered an Uber to get as close to the protest as I could. The MPD were redirecting traffic and were protecting/surveilling the peaceful protests with helicopters, motorcycles, and SUVs. The protesters carried signs that reflected a nationwide discourse: "Trump is not our president." I joined a group of people and spoke to several members of the activist organizations present, including Dream Defenders. Nobody seemed to know how the protest had come together and told me that it had emerged "organically." One student had begun to voice her frustrations and had gathered support earlier that evening. People had recorded it with their cell phones, and social media had done the rest.

Before the protest ended, back in Downtown Miami, I had been walking behind a man who was carrying a sign that read, "Trump does not represent American values." I took a picture of him and his sign (see figure C.1). I looked at the photo and wondered to what extent my findings in Miami were shaped by larger national values. As Ta-Nehisi Coates (2017) notes, we might understand Trump as "the first white president," who explicitly used his whiteness in his campaign and presidency as a way to mobilize support. In both speech and practice, Trump appeared concerned with "white suffering": the idea that white people (and especially white men) are under threat by nonwhite people: culturally, economically, and physically—mostly through crime and violence. In light of this perceived threat, Trump called for more law and order, and showed his unconditional support for the police and their violent and extralegal practices. Beyond his support for the police, Trump also fueled an individualized logic of security, encouraging citizens to become increasingly vigilant, to be mindful of their safety, and to protect themselves when necessary.

Numerous recent examples of racist and violent acts highlight how vigilant citizenship underlies broadly shared assumptions regarding citizen rights, duties, and responsibilities. In 2020, Kyle Rittenhouse shot three and killed two unarmed citizens during a BLM demonstration. A year later, the seventeen-year-old boy was acquitted of all charges. Not only because the legal system had—once again—failed to provide some form of justice, but also because of the blatant support Rittenhouse and his paramilitary group of vigilantes enjoyed throughout the United States. Politicians stated that he had had the right to defend himself, explaining that Rittenhouse had the right mindset and even offering him jobs. While it is already terrifying that his actions can be classified as a legal form of self-defense, the actions of the likes of Rittenhouse continue to be rationalized by a language that is deeply embedded in moral, political, and legal codes. A language that masks how his actions are actually part of a national discourse of what it means to be a good citizen in this country.

While vigilant citizenship helps to point out the structural conditions of such extreme violence, it also urges us to look past these acts as the only manifestation of white supremacy. In particular, it shifts our attention to the ways that racialized inequalities are part of everyday policing; as a way of living, and dealing, with perceived insecurities. Just a few months earlier in 2020, Amy Cooper, a white woman, called 911 when she encountered Christian Cooper (no relation), a Black man who was birdwatching in Central Park. When Christian had asked Amy to put her dog on a leash, she called the emergency number and told the dispatcher that an African American man was threatening her dog. Meanwhile, Christian took out his cell phone and recorded the interaction. The video went viral and eventually became a key illustration of the popularized notion of the "Karen"—a pejorative term for a white, privileged, and racist woman and policing actor. A "Karen" is someone, as Sherina Feliciano-Santos also points out, who acts to "police the acceptable bounds of Blackness in white public space" (2021: 262). While vigilant citizenship clearly skews male, the by-now mainstream notion of the "Karen" illustrates how both men and women have taken a central role in the everyday policing of Blackness.

To no surprise, Trump backed Kyle Rittenhouse during his trial and congratulated him on his acquittal: "If that's not self-defense, nothing is!" Trump wrote in a public statement. Trump is not the first president to recontextualize racist violence as a matter of self-defense. Yet Trump gave the central premise of vigilant citizenship an enormous boost in popularity and endorsement—not only through his political support of right-wing extremists and violence but also through his tacit endorsement of the internalization of self-protection in various aspects of everyday life (the latter, e.g., involving Trump suggesting teachers and school personnel be armed to deter future school shootings). In a sense, contradicting the Miami protester's sign, Trump *does* represent these national values.

While elected leaders obviously have a significant impact on policing, the individualized logic of security transcends party lines and presidencies. Ideals of private security, litigation, and lateral surveillance have become cornerstones of urban governance in the past decades, informing everyday practices and understandings of what it means to enact vigilant citizenship today. The main take away of this book is to convey the message that a logic of policing race is pervasive outside political bodies and institutions, beyond the reach of elected officials, where it is internalized and routinely employed by a broad range of actors. It is therefore the challenge for future leaders, as well as citizens in their everyday lives, to question such ideals and practices, to resist the urge to reinforce individualized solutions to insecurity, and to shift their attention to the sociological and structural issues masked by vigilant citizenship.

ACKNOWLEDGMENTS

I would like to thank all the Miamians who were willing to share their experiences with me, to introduce me to their livelihoods and show me around in a city I had never been to before. Over the course of almost a year, I became part of your lives and regularly accompanied you to work, to the cinema, to public meetings, to the veterinarian, to bars, and at home, where you shared your stories and even your secrets with me. Many of you experienced difficulties during my research. Because of stress or anxiety induced by work, relationships, or other issues (hopefully I wasn't a source of such), I am incredibly thankful for the time you took to involve me in your daily lives despite these concerns and feelings of precariousness.

I also like to thank the companies, organizations, and agencies that facilitated my research in Miami. As police departments are scrutinized throughout the United States and elsewhere, I am grateful that the Miami Police Department and Miami Beach Police Department were still open to the idea of having an external researcher look into their daily routines and training courses. I thank Xecurity (a pseudonym) and its helpful owner for introducing me to private security work, including Xecurity courses and shooting range. I thank Dream Defenders for being supportive of my research. It was a privilege to be part of the inspiring meetings and demonstrations that members of this civil-rights collective organized during important times for many Miamians.

Merel, my partner, was my essential and wonderful support in both her absence and presence. Thank you for everything: your empathy, love, patience, understanding, and intellect during my fieldwork in South Florida and over the course of writing this book. I am thankful to have Hans, Trudy, and Lotte as my family, for their unconditional support, enthusiasm, and determination to visit me wherever I go. Alfredo, it was great to study your hometown with you. Thank you for introducing me to Miami from day two, where we strolled and cycled through the streets of Wynwood for leisure and for work, listened to jazz at Lagniappe, traveled in and outside Florida, and enjoyed most of the good food and entertainment Miami has to offer. Thank you for inviting me to many events and to your family home, as well as for assisting me in finding the necessary contacts for my research. Kevin and Pieter, thank you for coming over and joining me during some necessary time off at the beach and the arcade.

Special thanks goes out to my editor at NYU Press, Jennifer Hammer, for her thoughtful comments and availability—for helping me throughout the process. Writing and revising a book is a daunting and challenging process, and particularly so when it is your first time. I am therefore grateful that Jennifer was always there to guide me during every step. Also essential have been the two anonymous readers who reviewed my manuscript multiple times. Thank you so much for the wonderful suggestions and comments on earlier versions of my book: your input has been invaluable and extremely appreciated. Thank you for all the time and dedication, and I hope the final product is to your liking. Feels weird I can never say thank you personally.

I thank my friends and (former) colleagues at the University of Amsterdam and Utrecht University. In particular, I thank Rivke, Carolina, Francesco, and Alana for being a collective of amazing researchers and individuals. Rivke: I have been so lucky to have you as a patient, engaged, and talented mentor—thanks for the professional and personal support to this very day. I will always look forward to working with you, and especially our writing and research days together. Rivke's Engelen (Rivke's angels): it was really special working and spending time together wherever. I have learned much more from you than I did from my own research (but don't tell anyone that). Alana and Tracian, thank you for accommodating me in Kingston, Jamaica, and for offering guidance in the midst of our exhausting fieldwork. Francesco and Carolina, thank you for enjoying camp no-sleep with me, for the hilarious texts during meetings, courses, and conferences, and most importantly, for always being there as friends. Timo, thanks for sharing your excitement for research. I hope there will be many more stories for us to make, tell, and share in the future.

Finally, I am thankful for being part of a great team of researchers and analysts at my current department at Utrecht University. Chris, Luuk,

Lauren, Jolle and all the others who taught me before and who I can now call my colleagues: thank you for your supervision and teaching prior to my work in Miami. I could not have written this book if it were not for the amazing MA program you are all part of. I consider it a privilege to be part of the team and look forward to working together, in both teaching and research.

NOTES

INTRODUCTION
1. Since my first name rhymes with "nice," as in Tys.
2. Names withheld to preserve anonymity.
3. I would like to thank an anonymous reader for their helpful phrasing.
4. Quote from an interview with Blanchfield, "Cops Who Touched Fentanyl."
5. In a debate with Donald Trump, Joe Biden used the "bad apple" theory, see, e.g., Epstein and Eligon, "Biden Said, 'Most Cops Are Good.'"
6. See Gloria, "'Gunshine State' Prepares to Issue"; and worldpopulationreview.com, "Gun Ownership by State 2021."
7. US Census Bureau, "QuickFacts Miami-Dade County, Florida."
8. Based on the US Census Bureau, as quoted in Viglucci et al., "History of Broken Promises."
9. Quoted in Rabin, "Miami Used to be a Murder Capital," 2018.
10. Quoted in Iannelli, "Crime in Miami-Dade," 2018.

1. PLACES AND PARTNERSHIPS OF POLICING
1. See, e.g., a "Neighborhood-O-Meter" of Miami-Dade, a map created by an anonymous user of Google Maps that has over a million views. Overtown is considered red, which classifies as "bad areas, poor aspect and very unsafe."
2. Quoted in a letter written by Thomas E. Perez, assistant attorney general, US Department of Justice, in 2013. The letter can be found at the US Department of Justice website (www.justice.gov).
3. This intersection between policing and urban housing policies and real-estate development can be understood as a broader form of "speculative policing." Based on her study of Amsterdam, Jaffe (2019) shows that the neighborhoods where the most repressive forms of policing take place are those with a high potential for urban renewal. In other words, police practices target potential criminals, which makes "property owners and corporate investors feel more comfortable taking financial risks" (Jaffe 2019, 449–50).

2. DO THE RIGHT THING
1. As I explained in the introduction, I often stood out in Miami. Often dressed in a white T-shirt and shorts, my appearance was very unlike those who lived in Mia's neighborhood and wore formal attire.

2 As Spike Lee says in the "Director's Commentary," part of the *Do the Right Thing* DVD release.

3. GUNS FOR THE GOOD GUYS

1 Based on research by the security.org team (2019), "City crimes involving guns: analyzing gun incidents in major U.S. cities."
2 Based on research done by the Centers for Disease Control and Prevention (2019), "Firearm mortality by state." cdc.gov.
3 The landlord, however, who came by the old house while we were there to show it to two potential tenants, emphasized that the neighborhood was not the "ghetto." As she explained to the couple, "This is unracist, but poor people just don't belong here."

4. LOOKING THROUGH THE LAW

1 As stated on "Legal Observer Training," ACLU Wisconsin, www.aclu-wi.org/en/community-engagement/legal-observer-training.
2 E.g., a growing number of crime experts and police departments use geographic information systems and predictive analyses to shift police emphasis toward targeting more precise locations and people. This shift reflects a broader embrace of metrics and data in policing, which in turn shapes socio-spatial differentiation in police deployment. Jefferson (2020) shows how these predictive-policing models combine crime statistics and socioeconomic data to estimate when and where different types of crime are most likely to occur. Police departments across the globe rely on digital and data-driven methods to improve accountability, hoping to distance themselves from claims of bias and racial profiling. While modern technology allows the police to combat crime in sophisticated, detail-oriented ways, Manning (2008) shows that police strategies and tactics have not been altogether as transformative as expected. While algorithms are useful in identifying spatial and temporal patterns, predictive-policing models might translate into additional surveillance and policing in certain neighborhoods, which in turn makes it more likely for crimes in those areas to be registered in the first place.

BIBLIOGRAPHY

Abrahamsen, Rita, and Michael C. Williams. 2011. *Security Beyond the State: Private Security in International Politics*. Cambridge: Cambridge University Press.

Akarsu, Hayal. 2020. "Citizen Forces: The Politics of Community Policing in Turkey." *American Ethnologist* 47, no. 1: 27–42.

Alexander, Michelle. 2012. *The New Jim Crow: Mass Incarceration in the Age of Colorblindness*. New York: New Press.

Álvarez, Camila, dir. 2013. *Right to Wynwood*. Vimeo documentary video, 21:34. Accessed September 4, 2014. https://vimeo.com/110682099.

Alvarez, Lizette. 2012. "As Hip-Hop Devotees Come in, Many Miami Beach Residents Prepare to Leave." *New York Times*. May 25, 2012. nytimes.com.

Auston, Donna. 2017. "Prayer, Protest, and Police Violence: Black Muslim Spiritual Resistance in the Ferguson Era." *Transforming Anthropology* 25, no. 11: 11–22.

Azoulay, Ariella. 2008. *The Civil Contract of Photography*. New York: Zone Books.

Beliso-De Jesús, Aisha M. 2020. "The Jungle Academy: Molding White Supremacy in American Police Recruits." *American Anthropologist* 122, no. 1: 143–56.

Beliso-De Jesús, Aisha M., and Jemima Pierre. 2020. "Introduction to Special Section: Anthropology of White Supremacy." *American Anthropologist* 122, no. 1: 65–75.

Beutin, Lyndsey P. 2017. "Racialization as a Way of Seeing: The Limits of Counter-Surveillance and Police Reform." *Surveillance & Society* 15, no. 1: 5–20.

Bittner, Egon. 1970. *The Functions of the Police in Modern Society*. Bethesda, MD: National Institute of Mental Health, Center for Studies of Crime and Delinquency.

Blanchfield, Patrick. 2017. "Ghosts of 2012." *n+1*. December 14, 2017. www.nplusonemag.com.

———. 2021. "The Cops Who Touched Fentanyl." *New Republic*. September 29, 2021.

Bloomberg. 2016. "The 10 Most Unequal Cities in America: The South Florida City is Neck and Neck with Atlanta and New Orleans." *Bloomberg*. October 5, 2016.

Bonilla, Yarimar, and Jonathan Rosa. 2015. "#Ferguson: Digital Protest, Hashtag Ethnography, and the Racial Politics of Social Media in the United States." *American Ethnologist* 42, no. 1: 4–17.

Boots, Denise Paquette, Jayshree Bihari, and Euel Elliott. 2009. "The State of the Castle: An Overview of Recent Trends in State Castle Doctrine Legislation and Public Policy." *Criminal Justice Review* 34, no. 4: 515–35.

Browne, Simone. 2015. *Dark Matters: On the Surveillance of Blackness*. Durham, NC: Duke University Press.

Butler, Judith. 1993. "Endangered/Endangering: Schematic Racism and White Paranoia." In *Reading Rodney King/Reading Urban Uprising*, edited by Robert Gooding-Williams, 15–22. New York: Routledge.
Caldeira, Teresa P. R. 2000. *City of Walls*. Oakland: University of California Press.
Calvert, Scott, and Dan Frosch. 2020. "Police Rethink Policies as Cities Pay Millions to Settle Misconduct Claims." *Wall Street Journal*. Updated October 22, 2020. wsj.com.
Campeau, Holly. 2015. "'Police Culture' at Work: Making Sense of Police Oversight." *British Journal of Criminology* 55, no. 4: 669–87.
Carey, Grace A. 2019. "Anthropology's 'Repugnant Others.'" *American Ethnological Society*. April 23, 2019. https://americanethnologist.org.
Carlson, Jennifer D. 2014. "States, Subjects and Sovereign Power: Lessons from Global Gun Cultures." *Theoretical Criminology* 18, no. 3: 335–53.
———. 2015. *Citizen-Protectors: The Everyday Politics of Guns in an Age of Decline*. Oxford: Oxford University Press.
———. 2020. *Policing the Second Amendment: Guns, Law Enforcement, and the Politics of Race*. Princeton, NJ: Princeton University Press.
Cattelino, Jessica R. 2004. "The Difference That Citizenship Makes: Civilian Crime Prevention on the Lower East Side." *Political and Legal Anthropology Review* 27, no. 1: 114–37.
Centers for Disease Control and Prevention. 2019. "Firearm Mortality by State." cdc.gov.
Clarke, Kamari M. 2009. *Fictions of Justice: The International Criminal Court and the Challenge of Legal Pluralism in Sub-Saharan Africa*. New York: Cambridge University Press.
Coates, Ta-Nehisi. 2017. "The First White President." *Atlantic*. October 15, 2017.
Comaroff, John L., and Jean Comaroff. 2009. "Reflections on the Anthropology of Law, Governance, and Sovereignty." In *Rules of Law and Laws of Ruling: On the Governance of Law*, edited by Franz von Benda-Beckmann, Keebet von Benda-Beckmann, and Julia Eckert, 31–60. Farnham, UK: Ashgate.
Connolly, N. D. B. 2014. *A World More Concrete: Real Estate and the Remaking of Jim Crow South Florida*. Chicago: University of Chicago Press.
Correia, David, and Tyler Wall. 2018. *Police: A Field Guide*. New York: Verso Books.
Croucher, Sheila L. 1997. *Imagining Miami: Ethnic Politics in a Postmodern World*. Charlottesville: University of Virginia Press.
Davis, Mike. 1990. *City of Quartz*. New York: Verso Books.
De Koning, Anouk, Rivke Jaffe, and Martijn Koster. 2015. "Citizenship Agendas in and beyond the Nation-State: (En)countering Framings of the Good Citizen." *Citizenship Studies* 19, no. 2: 121–27.
Diphoorn, Tessa G. 2015. *Twilight Policing: Private Security and Violence in Urban South Africa*. Oakland: University of California Press.
Donovan, James M. 2008. *Legal Anthropology: An Introduction*. Lanham, MD: AltaMira Press.

Dunbar-Ortiz, Roxanne. 2018. *Loaded: A Disarming History of the Second Amendment*. San Francisco: City Lights Books.
Dupont, Benoît. 2004. "Security in the Age of Networks." *Policing and Society* 14, no. 1: 76–91.
Engel, David M. 2016. *The Myth of the Litigious Society*. Chicago: University of Chicago Press.
Epstein, Reid J., and John Eligon. 2020. "Biden Said, 'Most Cops Are Good.' But Progressives Want Systemic Change." *New York Times*. August 19, 2020; updated April 20, 2021. www.nytimes.com.
Ewick, Patricia, and Susan S. Silbey. 1998. *The Common Place of Law: Stories from Everyday Life*. Chicago: University of Chicago Press.
Fan, Mary D. 2019. *Camera Power: Proof, Policing, Privacy, and Audiovisual Big Data*. Cambridge: Cambridge University Press.
Fassin, Didier. 2013. *Enforcing Order: An Ethnography of Urban Policing*. Cambridge: Polity Press.
Flechas, Joey, Charles Rabin, Maya Lora, and Linda Robertson. 2020. "Defund the Police: What Does It Mean, and How Are Miami-Dade Governments Reacting?" *Miami Herald*. Updated June 14, 2020. www.miamiherald.com.
Fuller, Chris. 1994. "Legal Anthropology, Legal Pluralism, and Legal Thought." *Anthropology Today* 10, no.3: 9–12.
Gainsborough, Juliet F. 2008. "A Tale of Two Cities: Civic Culture and Public Policy in Miami." *Journal of Urban Affairs* 30, no. 4: 419–35.
Garcia, Alfredo. 2017. "The Walls of Wynwood: Art and Change in the Global Neighborhood." PhD diss., Princeton University.
Garland, David. 2001. "Introduction: The Meaning of Mass Imprisonment." In *Mass Imprisonment: Social Causes and Consequences*, edited by Garland, 5–7. London: SAGE Publications.
Gillespie, Alex. 2006. "Tourist Photography and the Reverse Gaze." *Ethos* 34, no. 3: 343–66.
Gilmore, Ruth Wilson. 1993. "Terror Austerity Race Gender Excess Theater." In *Reading Rodney King/Reading Urban Uprising.*, edited by Robert Gooding-Williams, 23–37. New York: Routledge.
Gloria, Cat. 2019. "'Gunshine State' Prepares to Issue Its 2-millionth Permit to Carry a Concealed Weapon." *Miami Herald*. Updated April 10, 2019. www.miamiherald.com.
Glover, Erika. 2016. "Miami Gun Buyback Event to Help Reduce Gun Violence." NBC Miami. March 12, 2016. www.nbcmiami.com.
Goffman, Alice. 2014. *On the Run: Fugitive Life in an American City*. Chicago: University of Chicago Press.
Goldstein, Daniel M. 2010. "Toward a Critical Anthropology of Security." *Current Anthropology* 51, no. 4: 487–517.
———. 2012. *Outlawed: Between Security and Rights in a Bolivian City*. Durham, NC: Duke University Press.

Gooding-Williams, Robert. 1993. "Introduction: On Being Stuck." In *Reading Rodney King/Reading Urban Uprising*, edited by Gooding-Williams, 1–14. New York: Routledge.
Göpfert, Mirco. 2013. "Bureaucratic Aesthetics: Report Writing in the Nigérien Gendarmerie." *American Ethnologist* 40, no. 2: 324–34.
Gordon, Colin. 2019. *Citizen Brown: Race, Democracy, and Inequality in the St. Louis Suburbs*. Chicago: University of Chicago Press.
Gosin, Monika. 2019. *The Racial Politics of Division: Interethnic Struggles for Legitimacy in Multicultural Miami*. Ithaca, NY: Cornell University Press.
Graham, Stephen. 2012. "When Life Itself Is War: On the Urbanization of Military and Security Doctrine." *International Journal of Urban and Regional Research* 36, no 1: 136–55.
Grunwald, Michael. 2006. *The Swamp: The Everglades, Florida, and the Politics of Paradise*. New York: Simon & Schuster.
Gulasekaram, Pratheepan. 2010. "'The People' of the Second Amendment: Citizenship and the Right to Bear Arms." *New York University Law Review* 85, n. 5: 1521–80.
Haggerty, Kevin D., and Richard V. Ericson. 2000. "The Surveillant Assemblage." *British Journal of Sociology* 51, no. 4: 605–22.
Hall, Stuart, Chas Critcher, Tony Jefferson, John Clarke, and Brian Roberts. 1978. *Policing the Crisis: Mugging, the State and Law and Order*. London: MacMillan Education.
Hansen, Thomas Blom. 2006. "Performers of Sovereignty: On the Privatization of Security in Urban South Africa." *Critique of Anthropology* 26, no. 3: 279–95.
Harding, Susan. 1991. "Representing Fundamentalism: The Problem of the Repugnant Other." *Social Research* 58, no. 2: 373–93.
Hier, Sean P., and Josh Greenberg. 2009. *Surveillance: Power, Problems, and Politics*. Vancouver: University of British Columbia Press.
Hirschfield, Paul J., and Daniella Simon. 2010. "Legitimating Police Violence: Newspaper Narratives of Deadly Force." *Theoretical Criminology* 14, no 2: 155–82.
Hornberger, Julia. 2011. *Policing and Human Rights: Violence and Justice in the Policing of Johannesburg*. New York: Routledge.
Iannelli, Jerry. (2018). "Crime in Miami-Dade is Down Almost 10 Percent This Year." *Miami New Times*, November 27, 2018. miaminewtimes.com.
Isin, Engin F. 2008. "Theorizing Acts of Citizenship." In *Acts of Citizenship*, edited by Isin and G. M. Nielsen, 15–42. London: Zed Books.
Jackson, John L. 2015. "Lights, Camera, Police Action!" *Public Culture* 28, no. 1: 3–8.
Jaffe, Rivke. 2012. "Talkin' bout the Ghetto: Popular Culture and Urban Imaginaries of Immobility." *International Journal of Urban and Regional Research* 36, no. 4: 674–88.
———. 2019. "Speculative Policing." *Public Culture* 31, no. 3: 447–68.
Jefferson, Brian J. 2020. *Digitize and Punish: Racial Criminalization in the Digital Age*. University of Minnesota Press.
Johnson, Devon, Patricia Y. Warren, and Amy Farrell. 2015. "Introduction: Race, Criminal Justice, and the Death of Trayvon Martin." In *Deadly Injustice: Trayvon Martin, Race, and the Criminal Justice System*, edited by Johnson, Warren, and Farrell, 1–4. New York: New York University Press.

Júnior, Domício Proença, and Jaqueline Muniz. 2006. "'Stop or I'll Call the Police!' The Idea of Police, or the Effects of Police Encounters over Time." *British Journal of Criminology* 46, no. 2: 234–57.

Karpiak, Kevin G., and William Garriott. 2018. "Introduction: Disciplines, Fields, and Problems." In *The Anthropology of Police*, edited by Karpiak and Garriott, 1–20. New York: Routledge.

Kruse, Corinna 2015. *The Social Life of Forensic Evidence*. Oakland: University of California Press.

Larkins, Erika R. 2018. "Police, Hospitality, and Mega-event Security in Rio de Janeiro." In *The Anthropology of Police*, edited by K. G. Karpiak and W. Garriott, 139–152. New York: Routledge.

Larsen, Mike, and Justin Piché. 2009. "Public Vigilance Campaigns and Participatory Surveillance after 11 September 2001." In *Surveillance: Power, Problems, Politics*, edited by P. Hier and J. Greenberg, 187–202. Vancouver: University of British Columbia Press.

Lazar, Sian. 2008. *El Alto, Rebel City: Self and Citizenship in Andean Bolivia*. Durham, NJ: Duke University Press.

Leatherby, Lauren, and Richard A. Oppel Jr. 2020. "Which Police Departments Are as Diverse as Their Communities?" *New York Times*. September 23, 2020. nytimes.com.

Lee, Spike, dir. 2001. *Do the Right Thing*. Universal City, CA: Universal Pictures.

Linnemann, Travis, Tyler Wall, and Edward Green. 2014. "The Walking Dead and Killing State: Zombification and the Normalization of Police Violence." *Theoretical Criminology* 18, no. 4: 506–27.

Local 10 News. (2015a). "Get Them Off the Streets" (TV news item). Local 10 News. Broadcast on May 28, 2015.

Low, Setha. 2004. *Behind the Gates: Life, Security, and the Pursuit of Happiness in Fortress America*. New York: Routledge.

Mann, Michael, dir. 2006. *Miami Vice*. Universal City, CA: Universal Pictures.

Manning, Peter K. 1978. "The Police and Crime: Crime and the Police." *Sociologische Gids* 25, no. 6: 486–501.

———. 2008. *The Technology of Policing: Crime Mapping, Information Technology, and the Rationality of Crime Control*. New York: New York University Press.

Marvar, Alexandra. 2018. "Artist Derrick Adams Shows I-95's Impact on Black Miami." *Bloomberg*. 11 December, 2018. bloomberg.com.

Mazzei, Patricia. (2018). "N.R.A. Joins Questioning of Florida Sheriff in 'Stand Your Ground' Case." *New York Times*. July 31, 2018. www.nytimes.com.

McDonald, Brent, and Hillary Bachelder, dir. 2017. *The Rise of Body Cameras*. New York Times Times Documentaries. January 13, 2017. www.nytimes.com.

Merry, Sally E. 1990. *Getting Justice and Getting Even: Legal Consciousness among Working-Class Americans*. Chicago: University of Chicago Press.

———. 2012. "What Is Legal Culture? An Anthropological Perspective." *Journal of Comparative Law* 5, no. 2: 40–58.

Miller, Toby 1998. *Technologies of Truth: Cultural Citizenship and the Popular Media*. Minneapolis: University of Minnesota Press.

Mirzoeff, Nicholas. 2011. "The Right to Look." *Critical Inquiry* 37, no. 3: 473–96.
Mohl, Raymond A. 1989. "Shadows in the Sunshine: Race and Ethnicity in Miami." *Tequesta* 49: 63–80.
Morejon, Liane. (2015). "Boy, 10, Dead in Miami Shooting." Local 10 News. March 25, 2015. www.local10.com.
Mouhanna, Christian. 2007. "Le Miracle de la Sécurité, vu de l'Intérieur." *Mouvements* 4: 35–44.
Mulla, Sameena. 2014. *The Violence of Care: Rape Victims, Forensic Nurses, and Sexual Assault Intervention*. New York: New York University Press.
Mulvey, Laura. 1975. "Visual Pleasure and Narrative Cinema." *Screen* 16, no. 3: 6–18.
Mutsaers, Paul. 2019. *Police Unlimited: Policing, Migrants, and the Values of Bureaucracy*. Oxford: Oxford University Press.
Natapoff, Alexandra. 2009. *Snitching: Criminal Informants and the Erosion of American Justice*. New York: New York University Press.
Neocleous, Mark. 2000. *The Fabrication of Social Order: A Critical Theory of Police Power*. London: Pluto.
Newman, Andrew. 2012. "Gatekeepers of the Urban Commons? Vigilant Citizenship and Neoliberal Space in Multiethnic Paris." *Antipode* 45, no. 4: 947–64.
Nightingale, Carl H. 2012. *Segregation: A Global History of Divided Cities*. Chicago: University of Chicago Press.
Nijman, Jan. 2011. *Miami: Mistress of the Americas*. Philadelphia: University of Pennsylvania Press.
Obert, Jonathan. 2018. *The Six-Shooter State: Public and Private Violence in American Politics*. Cambridge: Cambridge University Press.
Pirie, Fernanda. 2013. *The Anthropology of Law*. New York: Oxford University Press.
Plummer, Ken. 2003. *Intimate Citizenship: Private Decisions and Public Debate*. Seattle: University of Washington Press.
Portes, Alejandro, and Alex Stepick. 1993. *City on the Edge: The Transformation of Miami*. Berkeley: University of California Press.
Portes, Alejandro, and Ariel C. Armony. 2018. *The Global Edge: Miami in the Twenty-First Century*. Oakland: University of California Press.
Pratt-Harris, Natasha C., Michael M. Sinclair, Cynthia Barbara Bragg, Nicole R. Williams, Kalfani Nyerere Ture, Belinda Davis Smith, Isiah Marshall, Jr., and Lawrence Brown. 2016. "Police-Involved Homicide of Unarmed Black Males: Observations by Black Scholars in the Midst of the April 2015 Baltimore Uprising." *Journal of Human Behavior in the Social Environment* 26, no. 3–4: 37789.
Punch, Maurice. 2003. "Rotten Orchards: 'Pestilence,' Police Misconduct and System Failure." *Policing and Society* 13, no. 2: 171–96.
Rabin, Charles. 2019. "Miami Used To Be a Murder Capital. Now, Not So Much, as Crime Rates Hit Historic Low. *Miami Herald*. Updated January 9, 2019. www.miamiherald.com.
Ralph, Laurence. 2019. "The Logic of the Slave Patrol: The Fantasy of Black Predatory Violence and the Use of Force by the Police." *Palgrave Communications* 5, no. 1: 1–10. https://doi.org/10.1057/s41599-019-0333-7.

———. 2020. *The Torture Letters: Reckoning with Police Violence*. Chicago: University of Chicago Press.

Raschig, Megan. 2018. "'You Don't Know That': Refusals of Community Policing and Criminalization in California." *Journal for the Anthropology of North America* 21, no. 1: 5–20.

Reeves, Joshua. 2012. "If You See Something, Say Something: Lateral Surveillance and the Uses of Responsibility." *Surveillance & Society* 10, nos. 3/4: 235–48.

———. 2017. *Citizen Spies: The Long Rise of America's Surveillance Society*. New York: New York University Press.

Richardson, Allissa V. 2020a. "Smartphone Witnessing Becomes Synonymous with Black Patriotism after George Floyd's Death." *The Conversation*. July 13, 2020. theconversation.com.

———. 2020b. "Why Cellphone Videos of Black People's Deaths Should be Considered Sacred, Like Lynching Photographs." *The Conversation*. May 28, 2020. theconversation.com.

Rios, Jodi. 2020. *Black Lives and Spatial Matters: Policing Blackness and Practicing Freedom in Suburban St. Louis*. Ithaca, NY: Cornell University Press.

Risør, Helene. 2010. "Twenty Hanging Dolls and a Lynching: Defacing Dangerousness and Enacting Citizenship in El Alto, Bolivia." *Public Culture* 22, no. 3: 465–85.

Rivero, Daniel. 2013. "Does Miami Beach Need a Reality Check on Racism?" WLRN Public Radio and Television. May 29, 2013. wlrn.org.

Robbins Collection, The. 2010. "The Common Law and Civil Law Traditions." Berkeley Law. www.law.berkeley.edu.

Rosa, Jonathan, and Vanessa Díaz. 2019. "Raciontologies: Rethinking Anthropological Accounts of Institutional Racism and Enactments of White Supremacy in the United States." *American Anthropologist* 122, no. 1: 120–32.

Rosen, Lawrence. 2006. *Law as Culture: An Invitation*. Princeton, NJ: Princeton University Press.

Ross, Rick. 2006. "Hustlin.'" *Port of Miami*. Slip-n-Slide, Def Jam, and Poe Boy.

Sarat, Austin. 1990. "'. . . The Law Is All Over': Power, Resistance and the Legal Consciousness of the Welfare Poor." *Yale Journal of Law & the Humanities* 2, no. 2: 343–80.

Savransky, Rebecca. 2015. "Mayor Calls for End to Mugshots Used in Target Training." *Miami Herald*. January 19, 2015. www.miamiherald.com.

Scheper-Hughes, Nancy. 2014. "The House Gun: White Writing, White Fears and Black Justice." *Anthropology Today* 30, no. 6: 8–12.

Security.org Team. 2019. "City Crimes Involving Guns." June 15, 2019. security.org.

Seigel, Micol. 2018. *Violence Work; State Power and the Limits of Police*. Durham, NC: Duke University Press.

Souhami, Anna. 2012. "Institutional Racism and Police Reform: An Empirical Critique." *Policing & Society* 24, no. 1: 1–21.

Sontag, Susan. 2003. *Regarding the Pain of Others*. New York: Farrar, Straus & Giroux.

Steinmetz, Kevin F., Brian P. Schaefer, and Howard Henderson. 2016. "Wicked Overseers: American Policing and Colonialism." *Sociology of Race and Ethnicity* 3, no. 1: 68–81.

Stoughton, Seth W. 2016. "Principled Policing: Warrior Cops and Guardian Officers." *Wake Forest Law Review* 51: 611–76.

Tagg, John. 1988. *The Burden of Representation: Essays on Photographies and Histories*. Minneapolis: University of Minnesota Press.

Tate, Julie, Jennifer Jenkins, and Steven Rich. 2022. "1,042 People Have Been Shot and Killed by Police in the Past Year." *Washington Post*. Updated June 29, 22. washingtonpost.com.

Trnka, Susanna, and Catherine Trundle. 2014. "Competing Responsibilities: Moving Beyond Neoliberal Responsibilisation." *Anthropological Forum* 24, no. 2: 136–53.

Ture, Kalfani, and Anthony Angelo Gualteri. 2017. "Baltimore and Beyond: Racialized Ghettos, Violence, and the Role of Anthropology." *Transforming Anthropology* 25, no. 1: 3–10.

Urry, John, and Jonas Larsen. 2011. *The Tourist Gaze 3.0*. London: SAGE Publications.

US Census Bureau. 2019. "QuickFacts Miami-Dade County, Florida." Census.gov.

US Department of Justice. 2013. "Personal Firearms Record (ATF P 3312.8)." www.atf.gov/firearms/docs/guide/personal-firearms-record-atf-p-33128.

US LawShield. 2018. "About Us." USlawshield.com/about-us-2/.

Van Maanen, John. 1978. "The Asshole." In *Policing: A View from the Street*, edited by P. K. Manning and J. Van Maanen, 221–38. Long Grove, [IL]: Waveland Press.

Viglucci, Andres, Isaiah Smalls II, Rob Wile, and Yadira Lopez. 2020. "'A History of Broken Promises': Miami Remains Separate and Unequal for Black Residents." *Miami Herald*. Updated October 17, 2020. www.miamiherald.com.

Vitale, Alex S. 2017. *The End of Policing*. Brooklyn: Verso Books.

Von Benda-Beckmann, Franz, Keebet von Benda-Beckmann, and Julia Eckert, eds. 2009. *Rules of Law and Laws of Ruling: On the Governance of Law*. Farnham, UK: Ashgate.

Wacquant, Loïc. 2001. "The Penalisation of Poverty and the Rise of Neo-Liberalism." *European Journal on Criminal Policy and Research* 9, no. 4: 401–12.

Ward, Kevin. 2007. "Business Improvement Districts: Policy Origins, Mobile Policies and Urban Liveability." *Geography Compass* 1, no. 3: 657–72.

Ward, LaCharles. 2018. "'Keep Runnin' Bro': Carrie Mae Weems and the Visual Act of Refusal." *Black Camera* 9, no. 2: 82–109.

White, Michael D., Lisa M. Dario, and John A. Shjarback. 2019. "Assessing dangerousness in policing." *Criminology & Public Policy* 18, no. 3: 11-35.

Wood, Stacey E. 2017. "Police Body Cameras and Professional Responsibility: Public Records and Private Evidence." *Preservation, Digital Technology & Culture* 46, no. 1: 41–51.

World Population Review. 2021. "Gun Ownership by State 2021." Worldpopulationreview.com.

INDEX

Page numbers in *italics* indicate Figures.

ACLU. *See* American Civil Liberties Union
Adams, Derrick, 60
Adams, James, 36
Agnew, Philip, 22
Akarsu, Hayal, 12
Allapattah, 34, 64
American Civil Liberties Union (ACLU), 57, 59, 125
apartheid, 17–18, 150
AR-15, 101, 119
Arbery, Ahmaud, 9
Armony, Ariel C., 16, 35
Azoulay, Ariella, 141

bad-apple explanation, 11, 161n5
Beutin, Lyndsey P., 126
BID. *See* Business Improvement District
Black Lives Matter (BLM), 6; cameras used by, 138, 150; against police, 7; protests by, 30. *See also* Dream Defenders
Black people: incarceration rates for, 97; internalized racism of, 42–43; in Miami, 17–18, 22, 92; in MPD, 41–42, 47–48, 52–53; police brutality against, 8, 11; as problematic gun owners, 106; violence against, 9
Black witnessing, 141
Blanchfield, Patrick, 116
BLM. *See* Black Lives Matter
Blue Lives Matter, 6

body cameras, 122–23, 150; advertisements for, 133; police officers against, 129–31; police officers for, 131–32; *The Rise of Body Cameras* on, 137–38
Bonilla, Yarimar, 138
Brown, Michael, 9, 9–10, 61
bureaucratic aesthetics, 136
Bushey, James, 108
Business Improvement District (BID): definition of, 49; MPD and, 51–52; off-duty police officers and, 48; in Wynwood, 27, 48–50
Butler, Judith, 127

Caldeira, Teresa, 50
cameras, 15; for accountability, 133, 162n2 (chap. 4); arrests recorded with, 121–22; Black witnessing through, 141; BLM use of, 138, 150; citizenship reformulated through, 141; as empowering, 126; enabling looking otherwise, 139–44; individual liability and, 124; legal potentiality of, 128–33; as objective, 125, 141–42; personal cameras, 134–35, 143, 150, 153; personal testimony with, 125; photographic performance through, 134–38; police recorded with, 124–28, 139–40; in policing, 129–30; in vigilant citizenship, 123–24, 144. *See also* body cameras
Campeau, Holly, 28
Carey, Grace, 23
Carlson, Jennifer, 12–13

171

car theft, 95–96, 117
Chauvin, Derek, 30
Citizen, 145, 153; *Citizen Protect* in, 146–47; vigilant citizenship promoted by, 146, 149; as *Vigilante*, 147
citizen mobilization, 67, 69
citizenship: differentiations of, 140–41; good, 4, 67, 73; "saying something" in, 72; slice of, 72–80, 74, 78
Citizens on Patrol (COP), 63; as citizen mobilization, 67; conflicting interests of, 78; identification for, 64; patrols by, 64–65; program of, 65–66; training for, 66–67; worksheet for, 64
City on the Edge (Portes and Stepick), 16
civilian observers, 1–2
Clark, Stephen, 60
Clarke, Kamari Maxine, 143
Coates, Ta-Nehisi, 155
Coconut Grove: crime-watch group in, 73–75, 78–79; roadside rampage in, 75
Colina, Jorge, 19
Comaroff, Jean, 124
Comaroff, John L., 124
community policing, 28
Connolly, Nathan B., 17–18, 60
Cooper, Amy, 155–56
Cooper, Christian, 155–56
COP. *See* Citizens on Patrol
copspeak, 126, 143
CopWatch, 124–25
Correia, David, 126
cover your ass (CYA), 138
crime: in Miami, 19; politics shaping, 35–36; typologies of, 35; victimization in, 117–18. See also *Citizen*
Crime Stoppers, 81, 93
crime-watch group: in Coconut Grove, 73–75, 78–79; fear in, 75–76; MPD and, 74, 76; racism in, 75; threats against, 77
Croucher, Sheila, 17
Cuban Americans, 16–17
CYA. *See* cover your ass

Davis, Mike, 50
Department of Justice (DOJ), US, 39, 97–98
deputized citizens, 9
Díaz, Vanessa, 5
DOJ. *See* Department of Justice, US
Do the Right Thing, 92, 162n2 (chap. 2)
Do the Right Thing (DTRT): award ceremony for, 72–73; coupon from, 73, 74; funding for, 73
Dream Defenders, 22; aims of, 142, 144; protest by, 9–10; rally organized by, 60–61; survival skills course by, 116–17; at Trump protest, 154
DTRT. *See* Do the Right Thing

Eason, Marlon: document distributed for, 81, 82; information search for, 63, 80–81, 93; killing of, 80; vigil for, 86–87, 87
Eckert, Julia, 124
Estes, Mark, 102
Ewick, Patricia, 123

Fassin, Didier, 24–25
Feldman, Allen, 128
Feliciano-Santos, Sherina, 156
Flagler, Henry, 17–18
Florida: concealed-carry license in, 99; gun deaths in, 98–99; gun ownership in, 15, 97–99; gun regulations in, 99, 106, 119; "Never Again" movement in, 118–19; "shall-issue" legislation in, 99; voting in, 154
Floyd, George, 30, 133

Gainsborough, Juliet, 18–19
Garner, Eric, 9
Garriott, William, 7
gendered practices, 10–11, 156
Gilmore, Ruth Wilson, 128
Göpfert, Mirco, 136
Graham, Stephen, 102
Greenberg, Josh, 12

Grunwald, Michael, 17
Gualteri, Anthony Angelo, 140–41
gun-buybacks, 105–6
guns: AR-15, 101, 119; buybacks of, 105–6; concealed-carry license for, 99; differentiated ownership of, 103–6, *104*; as entrenched in US, 116; in Florida, 15, 97–99, 119; leaving behind the, 117–19; meaning and status of, 97; in Netherlands, 21; NRA on, 98, 101–2, 106; as personal, 152–53; regulations for, 31, 96–97, 99, 101–2, 106, 109–10, 118–19; of security guard, 88–91; among sheep and wolves, 98–102; shotguns, 95–96, 100–101; as stolen, 97–98; in US, 98; in vigilant citizenship, 15, 31; Wynwood store for, 99–101, 103–4, *104*, 110, 152. *See also* private gun ownership
gun violence: accountability in, 114–15; change from, 116; in everyday policing, 111–17; as expected, 115–16; in Florida, 98–99; normalization of, 115–16; by police, 113–14; recording of, 119; use-of-force continuum and, 112. *See also* lethal force; police brutality

HAC. *See* Housing Assistance Center
Haitian Americans, 16, 22, 89, 154
Hall, Stuart, 11
Hansen, Thomas Blom, 122
Harding, Susan, 23
hard laws, 104–5
Hernandez, Israel "Reefa," 9, 9–10
Hier, Sean P., 12
Hornberger, Julia, 135
Housing Assistance Center (HAC), 40, 128–29

Jackson, John L., 126
Jefferson, Brian J., 162n2 (chap. 4)
Jeursen, Thijs: attire of, 76, 161n1 (chap. 2); as "European" ethnographer, 20–29; pronunciation of, 2, 161n1 (Intro.); on ride-alongs, 1–3
Jim Crow, 12
Jones, Gareth A., 28–29
Jones, Marshae, 115–16

"Karen," 156
Karpiak, Kevin G., 7
King, Rodney, 126–27, 133
Kruse, Corinna, 132

Larkins, Erika Robb, 61–62
lateral surveillance, 15, 30–31, 148; beyond, 91–94; downsides of, 68, 149; as good citizenship, 67–68, 149; neighborhood-watch groups in, 67; popularity of, 70; state agencies and, 70; tensions in, 91; US laws for, 72
Latinx people, 7; in Allapattah, 34, 64; incarceration rates for, 97; in Miami, 16, 22, 154; in MPD, 41–42; in neighborhood-watch groups, 75–76, 78–80; as problematic gun owners, 106
lawfare, 124
laws: entitlement in, 123; fiction of justice with, 143; for guns, 31, 96–97, 101–2, 109–10, 118–19; for guns in Florida, 99, 106, 119; hard laws, 104–5; for lateral surveillance, 72; for private gun ownership, 31, 96–97, 104–6, 119; soft laws, 104–6; stand-your-ground, 8–9, 68–69, 119; visual documentation and, 124
Lee, Spike, 92, 162n2 (chap. 2)
legal observers, 125
lethal force: citizen use of, 8–9, 96–97, 118; legality of, 109–10; police officer use of, 108
Llanes, Rodolfo, 76, 80–81, 114

Manning, Peter K., 135, 162n2 (chap. 2)
Marjory Stoneman Douglas High School shooting, 118–19

Martin, Trayvon: killing of, 8–9; mural tombstone for, 9, 10; reflecting on, 116; stand-your-ground law and, 68–69
MAT. *See* Medication-Assisted Treatment program
MBPD. *See* Miami Beach Police Department
McDuffie, Arthur, 19–20
McDuffie riots, 19–20
Medication-Assisted Treatment (MAT) program, 40
Meggitt simulations, 111–12
Memorial Day weekend: ACLU at, 57, 59, 125; negative reputation of, 56; off-duty police officers in, 55; policing practices during, 57, 61–62; preparation for, 56–57, 58; shooting during, 56, 59
Merry, Sally Engle, 123
Miami: apartheid in, 17–18, 150; Black population in, 17–18, 22; budgets in, 39–40; business opportunities in, 16; car theft in, 95–96, 117; crime in, 19; Cubans in, 16; as divided, 18–19; ethnic politics in, 17; financial settlements in, 114; "Get Them Off the Streets" in, 70–71; gun-buybacks in, 105–6; Haitian Americans in, 16, 22, 89, 154; imagining of, 16–20; inequalities in, 3–4, 148; insecurity in, 62; Latinx people in, 16, 22, 154; Liberty City in, 105; map of, 38; migrants in, 16, 153; police brutality in, 42; policing districts in, 39; population in, 16–17; private detectives in, 26; private security companies in, 27–28; protest in, 154–55; public services in, 39–40; real estate market in, 17; resident security measures in, 8; riots in, 19–20; socio-spatial inequalities in, 35–36; transience in, 153; transportation in, 23–24; Trump election reaction in, 153–54; vigilant citizenship in, 13, 62. *See also* Allapattah; Coconut Grove; Overtown; South Beach; Wynwood
Miami Beach: HAC in, 40; homeless outreach program in, 40, 128–29; neighborhood-watch in, 76, 79; policing districts in, 39; private security in, 53–60, 58; as safe, 117–18; Washington Avenue police station in, 1. *See also* Memorial Day weekend; South Beach
Miami Beach Police Department (MBPD): "European" ethnography of, 20–29; fieldwork with, 20–21; liability and, 25; Memorial Day shifts for, 57; in Memorial Day weekend, 56; ride-alongs with, 1–3; second officer for, 129; shooting by, 56, 59; Washington Avenue police station for, 1
Miami Police Department (MPD), 3, 63; BID and, 51–52; Black officers in, 41–42, 47–48, 52–53; on car theft, 96; community-relations officer in, 65–66; crime-watch group and, 74, 76; CYA in, 138; demographics of, 41–42; diversity training for, 45–46; DOJ investigation of, 39, 161n2 (chap. 1); DTRT award ceremony at, 72–73; "European" ethnography of, 20–29; fieldwork with, 20–21; intentional shootings by, 39; Latinx people in, 41–42; liability and, 25; neighborhoods walks by, 44–45; off-duty officers in, 48; on Overtown, 34–35; racism in, 139–40; recruits for, 44–45; ride-alongs with, 3; surveillance and harassment by, 46–47. *See also* Citizens on Patrol
Miami Vice, 71–72
Miami World Center, 36–37
Mohl, Raymond A., 22
Mouhanna, Christian, 24–25
MPD. *See* Miami Police Department
Mulla, Sameena, 132
mural tombstone, 9, 10

National Black Police Association (NBPA), 136–37
National Center for Health Statistics, 98–99
National Rifle Association (NRA), 97; against gun research, 98; influencing gun policy, 101–2, 106
NBPA. *See* National Black Police Association
neighborhood-watch groups: in lateral surveillance, 67; Latinx people in, 75–76, 78–80; in Miami Beach, 76, 79; vigilance in, 92; Zimmerman in, 8–9
Neocleous, Mark, 108–9, 130
neoliberalism, 10
Netherlands: guns in, 21; Jeursen from, 2; police in, 21–22; US stereotypes in, 21
"Never Again" movement, 118–19
Newman, Andrew, 12
Nijman, Jan, 153
1984 (Orwell), 69
normative whiteness, 68
NRA. *See* National Rifle Association

Oates, Daniel, 25, 53
Obert, Jonathan, 91
off-duty police officers: in bars, 53, 55; *vs.* security guards, 48–49, 55; in Wynwood, 48–51
O'Neal, Paul, 137–38
Orwell, George, 69
Overtown: barbershop in, 43, 45, 103–4, 139–40, 150; Black police precinct in, 42; as "Colored Town," 17–18, 36, 44; community walks in, 44–45; crime-watch meeting in, 81–82; Culmer Park shooting in, 113–15; as dangerous, 34–35, 161n1 (chap. 1); establishment of, 17–18; information search in, 63, 80–81; local drug market in, 83–86; map of, 38; "mayor" of, 114–15; MPD on, 34–35; MPD outreach in, 80–81; NBPA in, 136–37; playground in, 60; police in, 39–47; policing of, 43–44; protest in, 33, 36–37; residents difficult in, 34; shop next door in, 80–87; voters in, 154; white man in, 24

Perez, Thomas E., 161n2 (chap. 1)
photographic performance, 135
Plummer, Ken, 152
police: gun violence by, 111–17; mug shots for target practice by, 20; in Netherlands, 21–22; in Overtown, 39–47; public complaints and, 41; as racialized and violent institution, 7; recording of, 124–28, 144; scrutiny of, 24–25
police brutality, 151; bad-apple explanation in, 11, 161n5; against Black people, 8, 11; debate over, 6; as everyday threat, 116–17; killings in, 8; lawsuits about, 133; legality and, 107–9, 128; in Miami, 42; in Netherlands, 21–22; qualified immunity and, 110; as racialized, 8, 11, 127; recording of, 122–23, 143; scholarship on, 4–5; use-of-force continuum in, 112
police culture, 28
police officers: against body cameras, 129–31; boundaries for, 5; bureaucratic aesthetics of, 136; on citizen categories, 101; fear in, 5; lethal force used by, 108; Meggitt simulations for, 111–12; personal cameras used by, 134–35, 143; personal weapons of, 13; photographic performance by, 134–38; preferential treatment for, 52; for private gun ownership, 101–2; qualified immunity for, 110; safety concerns of, 7–8; shooting policies for, 109–10; types of, 28; use-of-force continuum for, 112; vigilant citizenship and, 5–6; as violence workers, 11; as white, 41–42. *See also* off-duty police officers

policing: binaries in, 23; cameras in, 129–30; colonial character of, 11–12, 21; discretion in, 130; as dramaturgical performance, 135; "European" ethnography of, 20–29; everyday policing, 11–13; gendered practices in, 10–11; gun violence in, 111–17; inequality and insecurity in, 60–62; institutionalized racialization of, 20; as intentional, 151–52; intimacy in, 32; legality and, 107–9; nonstate actors in, 12; as public health issue, 7; racial caste system in, 12; racial disparities in, 8, 42–43, 152; racialized imaginaries in, 11; slave patrols and, 8; in South Beach, 38–39; vigilant citizenship in, 5, 15

Portes, Alejandro, 16, 35

Pratt-Harris, Natasha C., 43

private gun ownership, 12–13, 15, 93; buybacks in, 105–6; differentiated citizenship in, 104–5; DOJ on, 97–98; for exclusion, 103; felony convictions and, 97; home ownership and, 103; laws for, 31, 96–97, 104–6, 119; in Netherlands, 21; NRA on, 97; police officers supporting, 101–2; for public safety, 100–101; racism in, 97, 102; self-defense legislation in, 110–11; as state violence, 102; in US, 98; white vigilantism and, 149–50

private security: in bars, 54; in Miami, 27–28; in Miami Beach, 53–60, 58; private detectives in, 26. *See also* security guards

protests: by BLM, 30; by Dream Defenders, 9–10; in Overtown, 33, 36–37; about Trump, 145, 154. *See also* McDuffie riots

public vigilance, 91; police relying on, 70–72; as socially destructive, 69–70; WWI campaigns for, 69

Punch, Maurice, 109

qualified immunity, 110

racial caste system, 12, 151–52

racism: antiracism movement against, 22; in crime-watch group, 75; in MPD, 139–40; in private gun ownership, 97, 102; vigilant citizenship and, 5, 31–32, 147–48, 151, 155–56

Ralph, Laurence, 8, 112, 133, 151

RAND Corporation, 98

Regalado, Thomas, 105

Reiner, Robert, 28

Richardson, Allissa V., 141

Right to Wynwood, 50

The Rise of Body Cameras, 137–38

Rittenhouse, Kyle, 9, 155–56

Rodgers, Dennis, 28–29

Rodriguez, Delbert "Demz," 9, 10

Rosa, Jonathan, 5, 138

Ross, Rick, 18

Rubio, Marco, 119

Sandy Hook Elementary School shooting, 116

Scheper-Hughes, Nancy, 105

Second Amendment, 96–97; on gun ownership, 99; vigilante groups and, 102

security guards, 27–28; in bars, 53–55; illegal weapons of, 88–91; licenses for, 88, 98; limitations of, 48; as observer, 88; *vs.* off-duty police officers, 48–49, 55; physical contact by, 55. *See also* private security

See Something, Say Something Act, 72

Seigel, Micol, 11

self-policing, 14–15

Severe, Fritz, 113–14

"sharking," 34

shotguns, 95–96, 100–101

Silbey, Susan S., 123

soft laws: definition of, 104–5; for gun control, 106

Sontag, Susan, 125
South Beach, 36; bars in, 53–54; hype in, 38; map of, *38*; policing in, 38–39
South Park, 111
speculative policing, 161n3 (chap. 1)
stand-your-ground law, 8–9, 68–69, 119
Steinmetz, Kevin F., 11
Stephen P. Clark Government Center, 60–61
Stepick, Alex, 16
surveillance: technologies for, 70; tension caused by, 86. *See also* lateral surveillance

Tagg, John, 132
Taser, 133, 142
Torres, Antonio, 113–14
Trnka, Susanna, 15
Trump, Donald J., 153; protest against, *145*, 154–55; Rittenhouse supported by, 156; whiteness used by, 155
Trundle, Catherine, 15
Turchin, John, 71
Ture, Kalfani, 140–41
Turkish National Police, 12

United States (US): antiracism movement in, 22; gun regulation in, 96–97; guns entrenched in, 116, 119; guns in, 98; laws for lateral surveillance in, 72; legal entitlement in, 123; Netherlands stereotypes of, 21; police killings in, 8; racial caste system in, 12, 151–52; toy gun buybacks in, 106; values of, *145*, 145–56; vigilantism in, 102; WWI public vigilance campaigns in, 69
use-of-force continuum, 112
US LawShield, 110–11

van Maanen, John, 101
vigilant citizenship: cameras used in, 123–24, 144; *Citizen* promoting, 146, 149; as "civic engagement," 12; definition of, 4, 14; distrust in, 147; as elaboration of citizenship agenda, 14; enacting and experiencing of, 13–14; gendered practices in, 10–11, 156; guns in, 15, 31; ideal of, 10; as intimate, 152; "Karen" in, 156; lateral surveillance in, 15, 30–31; as legal gray area, 79, 91; in Miami, 13, 62; neoliberalism and, 10; normative whiteness in, 68–69; police officers and, 5–6; in policing, 5, 15; racism and, 5, 31–32, 147–48, 151, 155–56; self-policing in, 14–15; self-protection in, 15–16; "snitching" in, 68, 82–83, 85, 93; in US, 102; vigilance and vigilantism in, 88–91
Vitale, Alex S., 39–40
von Benda-Beckmann, Franz, 124
von Benda-Beckmann, Keebet, 124

Wall, Tyler, 126
Ward, LaCharles, 143–44
witness protection program, 82–83, 86
Wood, Stacy E., 132
A World More Concrete (Connolly), 17–18
Wynwood: as attraction, 37–38, 49; BID in, 27, 48–50; development of, 49–50, 161n3 (chap. 1); gun store in, 99–101, 103–4, *104*, 110, 152; map of, *38*; mural in, *120*; mural tombstone in, *9*, 10; off-duty police officers in, 48–51; police killings in, 9–10; public-private partnership of, 47–53, 61; racialized police practices in, 52; *Right to Wynwood* about, 50; voters in, 154

Xecurity, 27, 54

Zimmerman, George: Martin killed by, 8; in neighborhood watch, 8–9; stand-your-ground law and, 68–69; vigilant citizenship legitimizing, 14, 69, 152

ABOUT THE AUTHOR

THIJS JEURSEN is Assistant Professor at the Department of Humanities at Utrecht University. Thijs works and publishes on policing, citizenship, and urban inequalities based on ethnographic research in the United States and the Netherlands. In terms of current research projects, Thijs focuses on relationships between criminal law and spatial inequality in Amsterdam, and he explores socio-spatial segregation and urban representation in digital media.

www.ingramcontent.com/pod-product-compliance
Lightning Source LLC
Chambersburg PA
CBHW020255030426
42336CB00010B/768